AI FOR RAILWAYS

Rakesh Kumar

In humble reverence to Lord Viswakarma, the divine craftsman and architect revered in the annals of Hindu mythology, we dedicate this book, "AI for Railways."

Lord Viswakarma, also known as Vishvakarman, is the epitome of craftsmanship, creativity, and ingenuity. As the divine architect of the devas, he embodies the spirit of innovation and excellence, guiding humanity towards the creation of magnificent marvels.

In ancient scriptures, Lord Viswakarma's presence is revered as the master artisan who fashioned the cosmos and crafted intricate celestial abodes for the gods. His divine craftsmanship knows no bounds, as he shapes the very fabric of existence with his skillful hands.

In contemporary Hinduism, Lord Viswakarma remains a beacon of inspiration for artisans, engineers, and creators across the world. His legacy transcends time and space, inspiring generations to strive for perfection in their craft and to embrace the spirit of innovation in all endeavors.

As we embark on a journey into the realm of artificial intelligence and railways, we invoke the blessings of Lord Viswakarma. May his divine guidance illuminate our path, empowering us to harness the power of AI to enhance railway operations, improve safety, and optimize efficiency.

With deepest reverence and gratitude, we dedicate this book to Lord Viswakarma, the divine craftsman whose timeless wisdom continues to inspire and guide us on our quest for excellence. Om Shri Vishvakarmaya Namaha!

CONTENTS

INTRODUCTION

In the ever-evolving landscape of transportation, railways have long stood as a cornerstone of connectivity, facilitating the movement of people and goods across vast distances with efficiency and reliability. As the demands on railway systems continue to grow, so too does the need for innovative solutions to enhance their operations, improve safety, and optimize efficiency. In this context, artificial intelligence (AI) emerges as a transformative force, offering a myriad of applications and opportunities to revolutionize the railway industry.

From predictive maintenance to passenger services and infrastructure management, AI technologies hold the promise of unlocking new levels of performance and sustainability in railway operations. By harnessing the power of machine learning, deep learning, natural language processing, and IoT-driven analytics, railways can not only address existing challenges but also pave the way for future advancements.

This book, "AI for Railways," delves into the intersection of artificial intelligence and railway operations, providing a comprehensive exploration of the various AI technologies, their applications, and their potential impact on the industry. Through a blend of theoretical insights, practical examples, and case studies, this book aims to equip readers with the knowledge and tools needed to navigate the evolving landscape of AI-driven railways.

The chapters within this book cover a wide range of topics,

starting with an overview of AI technologies and their importance in the railway sector. We delve into the historical development of railways and the fundamentals of railway operations, exploring key components such as infrastructure, signaling systems, and safety protocols.

Subsequent chapters delve into the applications of AI in railway operations, including predictive maintenance, automated train control, traffic management, and freight logistics. We examine real-world case studies and success stories, showcasing how AI is already transforming railway operations across the globe.

However, alongside the opportunities that AI presents, there are also challenges and ethical considerations to address. Throughout this book, we explore the regulatory frameworks, ethical guidelines, and emerging AI technologies shaping the future of railway systems.

Ultimately, "AI for Railways" serves as a guide for railway professionals, policymakers, and enthusiasts alike, offering insights into the transformative potential of AI and its role in shaping the future of transportation. Whether you're a seasoned industry veteran or a newcomer to the field, this book provides a roadmap for navigating the exciting intersection of AI and railways.

AI TECHNOLOGIES

AI technologies encompass a wide range of tools and methods aimed at enabling machines to perform tasks that traditionally require human intelligence. These technologies are rapidly evolving and finding applications across various industries, including transportation, healthcare, finance, manufacturing, and more. In the context of the railway industry, AI technologies hold significant promise for enhancing safety, efficiency, and passenger experience. Here's an overview of some key AI technologies:

1. Machine Learning (ML):
   Machine learning is a subset of artificial intelligence that focuses on developing algorithms capable of learning from data and making predictions or decisions without being explicitly programmed. It includes various techniques such as supervised learning, unsupervised learning, and reinforcement learning. In railway applications, machine learning algorithms can be used for predictive maintenance, anomaly detection, demand forecasting, and route optimization.

2. Deep Learning:
   Deep learning is a subfield of machine learning that uses artificial neural networks with multiple layers to extract higher-level features from raw data. Deep learning models, such as convolutional neural networks (CNNs) and recurrent neural networks (RNNs), have demonstrated remarkable performance in tasks such as image recognition, natural language processing, and time-series analysis. In railways, deep learning techniques are employed for tasks like image-based track inspection, text

analysis for incident reporting, and predictive maintenance based on sensor data.

3. Natural Language Processing (NLP):

NLP is a branch of artificial intelligence concerned with the interaction between computers and human language. It encompasses tasks such as text analysis, sentiment analysis, language translation, and chatbot development. In the railway industry, NLP technologies are used for customer service applications, including ticketing systems, automated announcements, and responding to passenger inquiries.

4. Robotics and Automation:

Robotics involves the design, construction, operation, and use of robots to perform tasks autonomously or with minimal human intervention. In railways, robotic systems can be deployed for track inspection, maintenance activities, and surveillance tasks. Autonomous vehicles, drones, and robotic arms are examples of robotic technologies used in railway applications to improve efficiency and safety.

5. Data Analytics and Big Data:

AI technologies heavily rely on data, and the railway industry generates vast amounts of data from various sources such as sensors, cameras, ticketing systems, and maintenance logs. Data analytics techniques, including statistical analysis, data mining, and visualization, are employed to extract insights, identify patterns, and optimize operations. Big data platforms enable the storage, processing, and analysis of large-scale datasets, facilitating the implementation of AI-driven solutions in railways.

6. Internet of Things (IoT):

IoT refers to the network of interconnected devices embedded with sensors, actuators, and software that enable them to collect and exchange data. In railways, IoT technologies play a crucial role in monitoring infrastructure, rolling stock, and passenger information systems in real-time. IoT sensors provide valuable data for predictive maintenance, condition monitoring, and improving operational efficiency.

Overall, AI technologies are transforming the railway industry by enabling smarter decision-making, automation of routine tasks, and proactive maintenance strategies, ultimately leading to safer, more efficient, and passenger-friendly rail transportation systems.

IMPORTANCE OF AI IN RAILWAY

The importance of AI in the railway sector cannot be overstated, as it brings forth a multitude of benefits and advancements that significantly impact safety, efficiency, and passenger experience. Here are some key aspects highlighting the importance of AI in the railway sector:

1. Enhanced Safety: Safety is paramount in the railway industry, and AI technologies play a crucial role in improving safety measures. AI-powered systems can monitor track conditions, detect potential faults or anomalies in real-time, and predict maintenance needs, thereby reducing the risk of accidents and ensuring the safety of passengers and railway staff.

2. Predictive Maintenance: Traditional maintenance practices often rely on fixed schedules or reactive approaches, leading to inefficiencies and unexpected breakdowns. AI enables predictive maintenance by analyzing data from sensors, equipment performance history, and environmental factors to anticipate maintenance requirements. This proactive approach minimizes downtime, optimizes asset utilization, and extends the lifespan of railway infrastructure and rolling stock.

3. Optimized Operations: AI algorithms can optimize various aspects of railway operations, including train scheduling, routing, and traffic management. By considering factors such as demand patterns, network capacity, and weather conditions, AI systems can dynamically adjust schedules and routes to

improve efficiency, reduce congestion, and minimize delays, leading to smoother and more reliable transportation services.

4. Improved Passenger Experience: AI technologies contribute to enhancing the overall passenger experience by providing personalized services, real-time information, and efficient ticketing systems. Chatbots powered by natural language processing (NLP) offer instant assistance to passengers, while AI-based recommendation systems provide personalized travel suggestions. Additionally, AI-driven analytics enable operators to anticipate passenger demand, optimize seating arrangements, and address customer feedback more effectively.

5. Cost Savings and Resource Optimization: By optimizing operations, reducing downtime, and improving maintenance practices, AI helps railway operators achieve significant cost savings and resource optimization. Predictive maintenance reduces the need for costly emergency repairs and minimizes the risk of service disruptions, while optimized scheduling and routing lead to more efficient use of rolling stock, infrastructure, and workforce resources.

6. Environmental Sustainability: AI can contribute to environmental sustainability initiatives in the railway sector by optimizing energy consumption, reducing emissions, and promoting modal shift from road to rail. AI-powered systems can optimize train speed, acceleration, and braking patterns to minimize energy consumption while maintaining operational efficiency. Additionally, AI-driven predictive analytics help identify opportunities for energy savings and emission reductions across the rail network.

7. Facilitation of Innovation and Research: AI fosters innovation and research in the railway sector by enabling the development of new technologies, tools, and methodologies. Researchers and engineers leverage AI to tackle complex challenges such as autonomous trains, smart infrastructure, and next-generation

signaling systems. The continuous advancement of AI opens up new possibilities for improving railway operations, safety, and sustainability.

In summary, AI is indispensable in the railway sector for its ability to enhance safety, optimize operations, improve passenger experience, achieve cost savings, promote sustainability, and drive innovation. As technology continues to evolve, AI will play an increasingly pivotal role in shaping the future of rail transportation worldwide.

HISTORICAL DEVELOPMENT OF RAILWAYS

1. Early Origins:
 - The origins of railways can be traced back to ancient civilizations where rudimentary forms of track-based transportation existed, such as the use of wooden rails or stone tracks to facilitate the movement of wheeled vehicles.

 - In the early modern period, advancements in mining and industrialization led to the development of wagonways and tramways in Europe for transporting goods over short distances, primarily in mining regions.

2. The Steam Era:
 - The invention of the steam engine in the 18th century by figures like James Watt and the subsequent development of steam locomotives by engineers like George Stephenson revolutionized transportation.

 - The opening of the Stockton and Darlington Railway in 1825 in England marked the beginning of the railway age, demonstrating the viability of steam-powered locomotion for transporting both passengers and freight.

3. Expansion and Innovation:
 - The 19th century witnessed a rapid expansion of railways worldwide, with major networks being constructed across Europe, North America, Asia, and other regions.

- Technological innovations such as the development of stronger rails, improved signaling systems, and standardized track gauges facilitated the growth of railway networks and increased operational efficiency.

4. Electrification and High-Speed Rail:
- The late 19th and early 20th centuries saw the electrification of railway lines in urban areas, leading to faster and more reliable commuter services.
- The introduction of high-speed rail in the latter half of the 20th century, starting with Japan's Shinkansen in 1964, transformed long-distance travel by rail, offering unprecedented speeds and comfort.

Current Trends in Railways

1. Technological Advancements:
- Railways are embracing digitalization and automation, with technologies such as artificial intelligence, IoT, and big data analytics being deployed to improve safety, efficiency, and passenger experience.
- Advancements in propulsion systems, including hydrogen fuel cells and battery-electric trains, are making rail travel more environmentally sustainable.

2. High-Speed Rail Expansion:
- High-speed rail continues to expand globally, with new lines being planned and constructed in regions such as Europe, Asia, and North America.
- Investments in high-speed rail aim to provide fast, reliable, and environmentally friendly alternatives to air and road travel for intercity transportation.

3. Sustainability and Green Initiatives:
- Railways are increasingly recognized as a sustainable mode of transportation, contributing to efforts to reduce greenhouse gas emissions and combat climate change.

- Initiatives such as electrification, energy-efficient rolling stock, and the use of renewable energy sources are being implemented to make railways even more environmentally friendly.

4. Intermodal Connectivity:
- Railways play a crucial role in promoting intermodal connectivity by integrating seamlessly with other modes of transportation, such as buses, trams, metros, and bicycles.
- Integrated transportation networks offer passengers greater flexibility and convenience in their journeys while reducing congestion and pollution in urban areas.

5. Expansion of Freight Rail:
- Freight railroads continue to be a vital component of global logistics networks, transporting goods efficiently and cost-effectively over long distances.
- Investments in freight rail infrastructure, including track upgrades and intermodal terminals, aim to enhance capacity, reliability, and safety in the movement of goods.

6. Urban Rail Development:
- Rapid urbanization has spurred investments in urban rail systems such as metros, light rail transit (LRT), and commuter rail networks to address growing transportation needs in cities.
- Urban rail projects focus on improving mobility, reducing congestion, and promoting sustainable urban development through compact, transit-oriented communities.

Overall, the historical development and current trends in railways reflect a dynamic and evolving industry that continues to innovate and adapt to meet the challenges and opportunities of the modern world.

FUNDAMENTALS OF RAILWAY OPERATIONS

The fundamentals of railway operations encompass a wide range of principles, practices, and procedures involved in the planning, management, and execution of railway services. These fundamentals are essential for ensuring the safe, efficient, and reliable movement of trains and passengers or freight. Here's an explanation of the key aspects of railway operations:

1. Network Planning and Design:
   - Railway operations begin with the planning and design of the railway network. This involves determining routes, track layouts, station locations, and infrastructure requirements to meet transportation demand while considering factors such as geography, population density, and economic viability.

2. Scheduling and Timetabling:
   - Scheduling and timetabling involve the creation of schedules for train movements, including departure and arrival times, stopovers, and connections between different services. Timetables must be carefully coordinated to optimize capacity utilization, minimize conflicts, and provide reliable service to passengers or shippers.

3. Train Dispatching and Control:
   - Train dispatching is the process of managing train movements to ensure safe and efficient operations. Dispatchers

monitor train positions, track conditions, and signals to regulate the flow of trains, prevent conflicts, and maintain schedule adherence. Advanced signaling and control systems facilitate real-time decision-making and communication between dispatchers and train crews.

4. Safety and Regulations:
- Safety is paramount in railway operations, and strict regulations govern every aspect of rail transportation to prevent accidents and ensure compliance with safety standards. Regulations cover areas such as track maintenance, signaling systems, train operations, crew training, and emergency procedures. Safety audits, inspections, and enforcement mechanisms are used to uphold safety standards.

5. Maintenance and Infrastructure Management:
- Maintaining railway infrastructure is essential for ensuring safe and reliable operations. This includes track maintenance, signaling maintenance, bridge inspections, vegetation control, and equipment maintenance. Regular inspections, preventive maintenance programs, and predictive maintenance techniques are employed to identify and address potential issues before they escalate into safety hazards or service disruptions.

6. Rolling Stock Management:
- Managing rolling stock (e.g., locomotives, passenger cars, freight wagons) involves maintenance, repair, and deployment of trains to meet operational requirements. This includes scheduling maintenance activities, monitoring equipment condition, and optimizing fleet utilization. Rolling stock management also encompasses procurement decisions, asset lifecycle planning, and compliance with regulatory standards.

7. Customer Service and Passenger Experience:
- Providing excellent customer service is essential for attracting and retaining passengers. Railway operators focus on improving passenger experience through amenities such

as comfortable seating, clean facilities, onboard entertainment, and accessibility features. Customer service representatives assist passengers with ticketing, reservations, inquiries, and complaints, ensuring a positive travel experience.

8. Performance Monitoring and Improvement:
 - Monitoring and analyzing performance metrics is critical for identifying areas of improvement and optimizing railway operations. Key performance indicators (KPIs) such as on-time performance, capacity utilization, reliability, and customer satisfaction are tracked and analyzed to assess operational efficiency and effectiveness. Continuous improvement initiatives aim to address bottlenecks, streamline processes, and enhance service quality.

9. Emergency Preparedness and Response:
 - Railway operators must be prepared to respond to emergencies such as accidents, natural disasters, or security threats. Emergency response plans outline procedures for evacuating passengers, coordinating with emergency services, and restoring operations following disruptions. Training programs ensure that staff are prepared to handle emergencies effectively and minimize risks to passengers and personnel.

Overall, the fundamentals of railway operations encompass a comprehensive set of principles and practices that govern the planning, management, and execution of rail transportation services. By adhering to these fundamentals and continuously striving for improvement, railway operators can ensure safe, efficient, and reliable operations that meet the needs of passengers and shippers while contributing to sustainable transportation systems.

RAILWAY INFRASTRUCTURE

Railway infrastructure refers to the physical components that make up a railway network, including tracks, bridges, tunnels, stations, signaling systems, electrification equipment, maintenance facilities, and other supporting structures. These elements collectively enable the safe, efficient, and reliable movement of trains and passengers or freight. Here's an explanation of the key components of railway infrastructure:

1. Tracks: Tracks form the foundation of a railway system and consist of rails, sleepers (ties), and ballast. Rails are long, parallel steel bars that support and guide the wheels of trains. Sleepers are placed horizontally beneath the rails to distribute the load and stabilize the track. Ballast, typically made of crushed stone or gravel, provides a stable foundation for the sleepers and facilitates drainage.

2. Bridges and Tunnels: Bridges and tunnels are structures that enable railways to traverse obstacles such as rivers, valleys, mountains, or urban areas. Railway bridges can vary in design, including beam, truss, arch, and suspension bridges, depending on factors such as span length and terrain. Tunnels are underground passages constructed through hills or mountains, allowing trains to pass through without altering the landscape.

3. Stations and Terminals: Stations and terminals are facilities where passengers board and alight from trains, and where services are coordinated and managed. They typically include

platforms, ticketing counters, waiting areas, restrooms, and other amenities for passengers. Terminals may also have facilities for freight handling, including loading docks and storage yards.

4. Signaling Systems: Signaling systems are used to control the movement of trains and ensure safe operations. They include various types of signals, such as fixed signals, color light signals, and electronic signals, which convey information to train operators about track conditions, speed limits, and upcoming hazards. Interlocking systems prevent conflicting movements and regulate the flow of trains at junctions and intersections.

5. Electrification and Power Supply: Electrification systems provide power to trains, allowing them to operate without relying on fossil fuels. Common types of electrification systems include overhead catenary wires, third rails, and battery-electric propulsion. Power supply infrastructure, including substations and transformers, distributes electricity to the railway network and ensures reliable operation.

6. Maintenance Depots and Yards: Maintenance depots and yards are facilities where trains and infrastructure are serviced, repaired, and maintained. They include workshops, equipment storage areas, inspection pits, and maintenance tracks. Maintenance activities may include routine inspections, repairs, overhauls, and upgrades to ensure the safety and reliability of the railway system.

7. Telecommunications: Telecommunication systems provide communication capabilities for railway operations, including voice communication between train crews and control centers, data transmission for signaling and control systems, and passenger information systems. Communication technologies such as radio, telephone, and GSM-R (Global System for Mobile Communications - Railway) enable real-time coordination and information exchange.

8. Environmental Considerations: Railway infrastructure design and operations take into account environmental considerations to minimize impacts on ecosystems, habitats, and communities. Measures such as noise barriers, wildlife crossings, and vegetation management help mitigate environmental impacts. Sustainable practices in construction, maintenance, and operations promote resource conservation and reduce carbon emissions.

Overall, railway infrastructure forms the backbone of a railway network, providing the physical framework for safe, efficient, and sustainable transportation. By investing in the development, maintenance, and modernization of infrastructure, railway operators can enhance service quality, improve reliability, and meet the evolving needs of passengers and freight shippers.

TRAIN SIGNALING SYSTEMS

Train signaling systems are critical components of railway infrastructure designed to control the movement of trains and ensure safe and efficient operations. These systems consist of various signaling devices, trackside equipment, and communication networks that provide information to train operators about track conditions, speed limits, and other relevant information. Here's an explanation of the key components and functions of train signaling systems:

1. Signals:
 - Signals are visual or audible indications displayed to train operators to convey information about track conditions and instructions for safe operation. They typically consist of lights, flags, or mechanical arms mounted alongside the track.
 - Signals are classified into different types based on their purpose and appearance. Common types of signals include:
  - Fixed Signals: These are stationary signals positioned at strategic locations along the track, such as approaching stations, junctions, or level crossings. They provide information about track occupancy and convey instructions to train operators.
  - Color Light Signals: These signals use colored lights (e.g., red, yellow, green) to indicate different aspects, such as stop, caution, or proceed. They are commonly used in modern signaling systems due to their visibility and flexibility.
  - Semaphore Signals: Semaphore signals use mechanical arms that are raised or lowered to convey information. They were widely used in older signaling systems but have been

largely replaced by color light signals in modern rail networks.

2. Interlocking Systems:
- Interlocking systems are mechanisms that prevent conflicting movements and regulate the flow of trains at junctions and intersections. They ensure that signals display safe aspects and routes are set correctly to prevent collisions or derailments.
- Interlocking systems use logic circuits and electrical or mechanical interlocks to coordinate the operation of signals, switches, and other trackside equipment. They are designed to enforce predetermined rules and safety principles to maintain safe separation between trains.

3. Track Circuits:
- Track circuits are electrical circuits installed along the track that detect the presence of trains by measuring changes in electrical conductivity. When a train occupies a track circuit, it shunts the circuit, causing a signal to indicate occupancy.
- Track circuits are used for train detection, occupancy detection, and broken rail detection. They provide vital information to signaling systems about the location and movement of trains, enabling safe and efficient operation.

4. Communication Networks:
- Communication networks facilitate communication between train operators, control centers, and trackside equipment. They enable real-time exchange of information about train movements, track conditions, and operational instructions.
- Common communication technologies used in signaling systems include radio communication, telephone lines, and dedicated communication networks such as GSM-R (Global System for Mobile Communications - Railway).

5. Safety Systems:
- In addition to signaling devices and trackside equipment,

signaling systems may incorporate safety systems to enhance operational safety and prevent accidents. These systems include:

- Automatic Train Protection (ATP) systems, which enforce speed limits and provide emergency braking if trains exceed authorized speeds.

- Train Control Systems (TCS), which monitor train movements and provide commands to enforce safe operation.

- Positive Train Control (PTC) systems, which use GPS technology to monitor train positions and prevent collisions or derailments.

Overall, train signaling systems play a crucial role in ensuring the safe and efficient operation of railways by providing essential information to train operators, coordinating train movements, and enforcing safety measures. These systems are continuously evolving with advancements in technology to meet the growing demands of modern rail transportation.

TRAIN CONTROL SYSTEMS

Train control systems are integral components of railway infrastructure designed to monitor and regulate the movement of trains along the tracks. These systems utilize a combination of technologies to ensure safe, efficient, and reliable operation of trains. Here's an explanation of the key components and functions of train control systems:

1. Automatic Train Protection (ATP):
   - Automatic Train Protection is a safety system designed to enforce speed limits and prevent trains from exceeding authorized speeds. It consists of onboard equipment installed in trains and trackside infrastructure such as signals and track circuits.
   - ATP systems continuously monitor the speed of the train and compare it against pre-defined speed profiles stored in the onboard computer. If the train exceeds the authorized speed limit, the ATP system activates emergency brakes to bring the train to a safe stop.
   - ATP systems may incorporate features such as overspeed protection, temporary speed restrictions, and emergency braking to ensure compliance with safety regulations and prevent accidents.

2. Automatic Train Operation (ATO):
   - Automatic Train Operation is a control system that automates train operation, including acceleration, braking, and speed control, without direct intervention from the train

driver. ATO systems rely on onboard sensors, computers, and communication networks to control train movements.

- ATO systems optimize train performance by adjusting acceleration and braking patterns to maintain consistent speeds, reduce energy consumption, and minimize travel times. They may incorporate algorithms for route optimization, schedule adherence, and energy-efficient operation.

- ATO systems can enhance safety by reducing the risk of human error, improving train handling, and maintaining precise control over train movements.

3. Positive Train Control (PTC):

- Positive Train Control is an advanced safety system that uses GPS technology to monitor train positions and prevent collisions or derailments. PTC systems provide real-time information about train locations, speeds, and movements to operators and control centers.

- PTC systems continuously compare train positions with trackside data to detect potential conflicts or hazards. If a train is at risk of exceeding authorized limits or violating safety rules, the PTC system initiates corrective actions, such as applying emergency brakes or issuing warnings to train operators.

- PTC systems can improve operational safety by providing proactive hazard detection, collision avoidance, and automatic intervention capabilities.

4. Communication-Based Train Control (CBTC):

- Communication-Based Train Control is a signaling system that uses wireless communication between trains and trackside equipment to control train movements. CBTC systems provide real-time data exchange between trains and control centers, enabling precise positioning and dynamic route management.

- CBTC systems use radio frequency or other wireless communication technologies to transmit commands, status updates, and operational instructions between trains and wayside equipment. This enables flexible and adaptive control of train movements, allowing for increased capacity and efficiency.

- CBTC systems are widely used in urban transit systems such as metros and light rail networks, where high-density operations and frequent stops require precise control and coordination of train movements.

Overall, train control systems play a critical role in ensuring the safety, efficiency, and reliability of rail transportation by providing precise control, monitoring, and intervention capabilities. These systems incorporate advanced technologies and safety features to optimize train operations and minimize the risk of accidents or disruptions.

SAFETY PROTOCOLS AND REGULATIONS

Railway operations safety protocols and regulations are comprehensive sets of rules, guidelines, and standards established to ensure the safety of railway operations, infrastructure, passengers, employees, and the general public. These protocols and regulations are enforced by railway authorities, government agencies, and regulatory bodies to mitigate risks, prevent accidents, and maintain the integrity of railway systems. Here are some key aspects of railway operations safety protocols and regulations:

1. Safety Management Systems (SMS):
   - Safety Management Systems are structured frameworks implemented by railway operators to proactively identify, assess, and mitigate safety risks throughout the organization. SMS typically include elements such as safety policies, risk assessments, safety training, incident reporting, and continuous improvement processes.

2. Infrastructure Safety Standards:
   - Railway infrastructure safety standards prescribe requirements for the design, construction, maintenance, and operation of railway tracks, bridges, tunnels, signals, electrification systems, and other infrastructure components. These standards address factors such as track geometry, structural integrity, signaling systems, fire safety, and accessibility.

3. Train Operations Procedures:
   - Train operations procedures define rules and protocols for train movements, signaling, speed limits, track occupancy, and emergency situations. These procedures ensure safe and efficient train operations by providing guidance to train operators, dispatchers, and other personnel responsible for managing train movements.

4. Occupational Health and Safety (OHS):
   - Occupational health and safety regulations establish requirements for the protection of railway employees and contractors working in various roles, including train drivers, maintenance workers, station staff, and construction crews. OHS regulations address hazards such as noise exposure, hazardous materials, manual handling, working at heights, and ergonomic risks.

5. Emergency Preparedness and Response:
   - Railway operators are required to develop comprehensive emergency preparedness and response plans to address various types of emergencies, including accidents, natural disasters, fires, medical emergencies, and security threats. These plans outline procedures for evacuating passengers, coordinating with emergency services, and restoring operations following disruptions.

6. Regulatory Compliance:
   - Railway operators must comply with applicable laws, regulations, and standards established by government agencies, regulatory bodies, and industry associations. Regulatory compliance ensures that railway operations meet minimum safety requirements and adhere to legal obligations related to safety, environmental protection, accessibility, and public welfare.

7. Risk Management:
   - Risk management practices are used to systematically

identify, assess, prioritize, and mitigate safety risks associated with railway operations. Risk assessments consider factors such as operational hazards, infrastructure integrity, human factors, environmental conditions, and regulatory requirements to develop risk mitigation strategies and control measures.

8. Training and Certification:

- Railway personnel are required to undergo training and certification programs to acquire the knowledge, skills, and competencies necessary to perform their duties safely and effectively. Training programs cover topics such as railway operations, signaling systems, emergency procedures, safety protocols, and regulatory compliance.

9. Safety Audits and Inspections:

- Regular safety audits and inspections are conducted to evaluate compliance with safety protocols, identify deficiencies, and implement corrective actions. Safety audits may be conducted internally by railway operators or externally by regulatory agencies, independent auditors, or industry associations to ensure accountability and transparency in safety management.

Overall, railway operations safety protocols and regulations play a crucial role in maintaining the safety and integrity of railway systems, protecting passengers, employees, and the public from harm, and promoting confidence in rail transportation as a safe and reliable mode of travel.

AI FOR PREDICTIVE MAINTENANCE

Applications of AI in railway operations for predictive maintenance involve leveraging machine learning algorithms and predictive analytics to anticipate equipment failures and schedule maintenance activities proactively. Here's how the process is typically done:

1. Data Collection and Integration:
   - The first step in predictive maintenance is to collect data from various sources within the railway infrastructure, including sensors, onboard systems, maintenance records, and historical performance data. This data may include information about equipment condition, operating parameters, environmental conditions, and past maintenance activities. Data integration involves aggregating and harmonizing data from different sources to create a unified dataset for analysis.

2. Data Preprocessing and Cleaning:
   - Raw data collected from sensors and other sources may contain errors, missing values, or inconsistencies that need to be addressed before analysis. Data preprocessing involves cleaning, filtering, and transforming the data to remove noise, fill in missing values, and standardize formats. This step ensures that the data used for predictive maintenance is accurate, reliable, and suitable for analysis.

3. Feature Engineering:
   - Feature engineering involves selecting and extracting relevant features from the dataset that are predictive

of equipment failures or maintenance needs. This may include engineering domain-specific features based on domain knowledge and expertise. Feature engineering aims to identify patterns, trends, and correlations in the data that can be used to train predictive models effectively.

4. Model Development:

- Machine learning algorithms, such as supervised learning, are used to develop predictive models that can forecast equipment failures and maintenance requirements based on historical data. Common machine learning techniques used for predictive maintenance include regression analysis, decision trees, random forests, support vector machines, and neural networks. These models learn patterns and relationships from the data and make predictions about future equipment performance.

5. Model Training and Validation:

- The predictive models are trained using historical data, where the input features are used to predict the target variable (e.g., time to failure, remaining useful life). Training involves optimizing model parameters to minimize prediction errors and improve accuracy. The trained models are then validated using separate validation datasets to assess their performance and generalization capabilities.

6. Deployment and Integration:

- Once the predictive models are trained and validated, they are deployed into production environments and integrated into existing railway maintenance systems and workflows. This may involve developing software applications or integrating predictive maintenance capabilities into existing enterprise asset management (EAM) systems. The predictive models generate actionable insights and recommendations that inform maintenance planning and decision-making.

7. Continuous Monitoring and Improvement:

- Predictive maintenance systems are continuously monitored and evaluated to ensure their effectiveness and reliability. Performance metrics such as prediction accuracy, false alarm rates, and maintenance cost savings are tracked over time. Feedback from maintenance activities and operational data is used to refine and improve the predictive models iteratively.

8. Adoption and Cultural Change:

- Successful implementation of predictive maintenance requires organizational buy-in and cultural change to embrace data-driven decision-making and proactive maintenance strategies. Training and education programs may be provided to personnel to familiarize them with predictive maintenance concepts and technologies.

By leveraging AI and predictive analytics for railway operations, organizations can optimize maintenance schedules, reduce downtime, extend asset lifecycles, and improve overall operational efficiency and reliability.

APPLICATIONS OF AI IN RAILWAY OPERATIONS FOR PREDICTIVE MAINTENANCE

Applications of AI in railway operations for predictive maintenance involve leveraging machine learning algorithms and data analytics to anticipate equipment failures and schedule maintenance activities proactively. Here are some specific applications of AI in predictive maintenance for railway operations:

1. Fault Prediction for Rolling Stock:
   - AI algorithms analyze sensor data from trains, such as vibrations, temperatures, and electrical signals, to detect anomalies indicative of impending equipment failures. By identifying patterns associated with specific faults or wear patterns, AI models can predict when components such as bearings, wheels, brakes, or traction systems are likely to malfunction.

2. Track and Infrastructure Monitoring:
   - AI-based systems process data from trackside sensors, cameras, and inspection vehicles to monitor the condition of railway tracks, bridges, tunnels, and other infrastructure

components. By detecting defects such as cracks, wear, or subsidence early on, predictive maintenance algorithms can schedule repairs or replacements before safety risks escalate.

3. Predictive Signal and Signaling Systems Maintenance:

- AI algorithms analyze data from signaling systems, including track circuits, interlockings, and signals, to detect anomalies or degradation in performance. By predicting potential failures in signaling equipment, railway operators can prioritize maintenance tasks and reduce the risk of signal failures, which can lead to disruptions or accidents.

4. Electric Traction System Maintenance:

- AI models analyze data from overhead catenary systems, substations, and electrical equipment to predict failures or malfunctions in electric traction systems. By monitoring parameters such as voltage, current, and insulation resistance, predictive maintenance algorithms can identify issues such as arcing, insulation degradation, or contact wire wear before they lead to service interruptions.

5. Predictive Maintenance for Switches and Crossings:

- AI algorithms analyze data from switch machines, point mechanisms, and track geometry measurements to predict failures or malfunctions in switches and crossings. By monitoring parameters such as switch position, rail alignment, and wear patterns, predictive maintenance systems can identify issues such as switch jams, broken components, or misalignments that can impede train movements.

6. Infrastructure Degradation Modeling:

- AI models use historical data on environmental factors, traffic loads, and maintenance activities to predict the rate of degradation and remaining useful life of railway infrastructure assets. By forecasting the deterioration of tracks, bridges, and other structures, railway operators can optimize maintenance strategies and allocate resources effectively to extend asset lifecycles.

7. Predictive Maintenance Scheduling and Optimization:

- AI algorithms optimize maintenance schedules by considering factors such as equipment condition, operational constraints, and resource availability. By analyzing historical maintenance data and operational patterns, predictive maintenance systems can generate optimal schedules that minimize downtime, reduce costs, and maximize asset availability.

8. Integration with Asset Management Systems:

- AI-based predictive maintenance solutions integrate with enterprise asset management (EAM) systems to streamline maintenance workflows and asset tracking. By providing real-time insights into equipment health and maintenance requirements, these integrated systems enable proactive decision-making and facilitate data-driven asset management strategies.

Overall, the application of AI in predictive maintenance for railway operations enables proactive maintenance strategies, improves asset reliability, and enhances operational efficiency, ultimately leading to safer and more reliable rail transportation services.

AUTOMATED TRAIN CONTROL SYSTEMS BY AI

Automated train control systems utilize artificial intelligence (AI) and advanced technologies to automate various aspects of train operation, including speed control, braking, acceleration, and route management. Here are some key applications of AI in automated train control for railway operations:

1. Automatic Train Operation (ATO):
   - ATO systems automate the operation of trains by controlling acceleration, braking, and speed based on predefined parameters and operational requirements. AI algorithms analyze real-time data from sensors, trackside equipment, and onboard systems to optimize train performance and ensure safe operation.
   - ATO systems improve efficiency by maintaining consistent speeds, reducing energy consumption, and minimizing travel times. They also enhance safety by reducing the risk of human error and maintaining precise control over train movements.

2. Train Traffic Management:
   - AI-based train traffic management systems optimize the flow of trains within railway networks by dynamically adjusting train schedules, routes, and speeds to minimize congestion and maximize throughput. These systems use predictive analytics to anticipate demand, identify bottlenecks, and optimize train

movements in real-time.

- Train traffic management systems improve operational efficiency, reduce delays, and enhance capacity utilization by balancing train movements and optimizing resource allocation across the network.

3. Automatic Train Protection (ATP):

- ATP systems use AI algorithms to enforce speed limits and prevent trains from exceeding authorized speeds. By continuously monitoring train positions, track conditions, and speed limits, ATP systems can detect potential hazards or violations and initiate corrective actions, such as applying emergency brakes or issuing warnings to train operators.

- ATP systems enhance safety by providing proactive hazard detection, collision avoidance, and automatic intervention capabilities to prevent accidents or derailments.

4. Collision Avoidance Systems:

- AI-based collision avoidance systems use sensors, cameras, and onboard computers to detect and track nearby trains, obstacles, and hazards in real-time. These systems analyze sensor data to assess collision risks and take evasive actions, such as slowing down, stopping, or changing routes to avoid accidents.

- Collision avoidance systems improve safety by providing early warning of potential collisions and assisting train operators in making timely decisions to mitigate risks.

5. Route Optimization and Planning:

- AI algorithms optimize train routes and schedules based on factors such as traffic conditions, infrastructure capacity, and operational constraints. These systems analyze historical data, demand forecasts, and real-time information to generate optimal routes that minimize travel times, reduce energy consumption, and optimize resource utilization.

- Route optimization and planning systems improve efficiency, reliability, and punctuality by minimizing delays, reducing conflicts, and optimizing resource allocation across the network.

6. Remote Train Control and Monitoring:

- AI-enabled remote train control and monitoring systems allow operators to remotely monitor train operations, adjust parameters, and intervene in emergencies from centralized control centers. These systems use AI algorithms to process data from onboard sensors, cameras, and communication networks to provide real-time situational awareness and control capabilities.

- Remote train control and monitoring systems improve operational efficiency, reduce labor costs, and enhance safety by centralizing control functions and enabling rapid response to incidents or emergencies.

Overall, the application of AI in automated train control for railway operations improves safety, efficiency, and reliability by automating train operations, optimizing traffic management, and enhancing decision-making capabilities. These systems enable railway operators to achieve higher levels of automation, performance, and service quality in managing train operations and delivering passenger or freight services.

TRAFFIC MANAGEMENT AND OPTIMIZATION

AI plays a crucial role in traffic management and optimization within railway operations by leveraging advanced algorithms and data analytics to improve efficiency, safety, and reliability. Here are some key applications of AI in this domain:

1. Dynamic Traffic Routing:
   - AI algorithms analyze real-time data, including train positions, schedules, and track conditions, to dynamically adjust train routes and schedules. By optimizing train movements based on current traffic conditions and operational constraints, AI systems minimize congestion, reduce delays, and improve overall network efficiency.

2. Predictive Maintenance Impact on Traffic:
   - AI-powered predictive maintenance systems forecast potential equipment failures and maintenance needs, allowing operators to proactively schedule maintenance activities during off-peak hours or low-traffic periods. By minimizing the impact of maintenance on train operations, AI helps maintain service reliability and punctuality.

3. Capacity Planning and Allocation:
   - AI algorithms analyze historical data, passenger demand forecasts, and operational constraints to optimize capacity planning and allocation across the railway network. By

dynamically adjusting train frequencies, capacities, and routes, AI systems maximize throughput while ensuring a balanced distribution of resources across different routes and time slots.

4. Real-Time Incident Detection and Response:
- AI-based monitoring systems analyze real-time data from sensors, cameras, and other sources to detect incidents such as track obstructions, signal failures, or equipment malfunctions. By automatically identifying and prioritizing incidents, AI systems facilitate rapid response and mitigation efforts, minimizing disruptions and maintaining operational continuity.

5. Energy Efficiency Optimization:
- AI algorithms optimize energy consumption by trains through predictive analytics and real-time control strategies. By adjusting train speeds, acceleration patterns, and regenerative braking systems based on energy demand forecasts and operational conditions, AI systems minimize energy usage while maintaining service levels.

6. Optimized Train Dispatching and Slot Allocation:
- AI-based dispatching systems optimize train scheduling and slot allocation to maximize network capacity and minimize conflicts. By considering factors such as train priority, resource availability, and track utilization, AI algorithms dynamically adjust dispatching decisions to optimize overall network efficiency and reliability.

7. Customer Experience Enhancement:
- AI systems analyze passenger data, including travel patterns, preferences, and feedback, to optimize service delivery and enhance the passenger experience. By providing personalized travel recommendations, real-time updates, and seamless connections, AI-powered systems improve customer satisfaction and loyalty.

8. Performance Monitoring and Continuous Improvement:

- AI-based performance monitoring systems track key performance indicators (KPIs) such as on-time performance, service reliability, and passenger satisfaction in real-time. By identifying trends, patterns, and areas for improvement, AI systems enable operators to implement targeted interventions and continuous improvement initiatives to enhance overall system performance.

Overall, AI-driven traffic management and optimization systems empower railway operators to improve operational efficiency, enhance safety, and deliver superior service to passengers and shippers. By leveraging advanced analytics and automation technologies, AI transforms railway operations, making them more adaptive, responsive, and resilient in meeting the evolving demands of modern transportation networks.

FAULT DETECTION AND DIAGNOSIS

AI has significant applications in fault detection and diagnosis within railway operations, leveraging advanced algorithms and data analytics to identify and diagnose equipment failures or anomalies. Here are some key applications of AI in this domain:

1. Anomaly Detection:
   - AI algorithms analyze sensor data from various components of railway infrastructure, such as tracks, signals, rolling stock, and electrical systems, to detect anomalies or deviations from normal operating conditions. By identifying abnormal patterns or behaviors in real-time data streams, AI systems can flag potential faults or malfunctions before they escalate into critical failures.

2. Predictive Maintenance:
   - AI-powered predictive maintenance systems analyze historical data, sensor readings, and maintenance records to forecast potential equipment failures or degradation. By identifying early warning signs of wear, corrosion, or other issues, predictive maintenance algorithms enable proactive scheduling of maintenance activities, reducing downtime and minimizing the risk of unexpected failures.

3. Signal and Signaling Systems Monitoring:
   - AI-based monitoring systems analyze data from signaling equipment, including track circuits, interlockings, and signals, to detect anomalies or irregularities in performance. By

continuously monitoring signal status, response times, and error rates, AI systems can identify potential faults or failures in signaling systems, ensuring safe and reliable train operations.

4. Rolling Stock Health Monitoring:
   - AI algorithms process data from onboard sensors, cameras, and diagnostic systems to monitor the health and performance of rolling stock components, such as traction systems, brakes, bearings, and wheels. By analyzing vibration patterns, temperature trends, and other indicators of equipment condition, AI systems can detect abnormalities or degradation in rolling stock components, facilitating timely maintenance or replacement.

5. Track and Infrastructure Inspection:
   - AI-powered inspection systems use image processing and computer vision techniques to analyze visual data from trackside cameras, drones, or inspection vehicles. By detecting defects such as track defects, rail cracks, or vegetation encroachment, AI systems can identify potential hazards or maintenance needs in railway infrastructure, enabling timely intervention and remediation.

6. Fault Diagnostics and Root Cause Analysis:
   - AI algorithms analyze sensor data, maintenance records, and historical performance data to diagnose faults and determine their root causes. By correlating symptoms with underlying issues, AI systems can identify the root cause of failures or malfunctions, enabling more effective troubleshooting and problem resolution.

7. Fault Localization and Isolation:
   - AI-based fault localization systems analyze sensor data and network topology to localize and isolate faults within railway systems. By identifying the precise location of faults or failures, AI systems facilitate targeted interventions and minimize the impact on overall system performance.

8. Real-time Monitoring and Alerts:

- AI-powered monitoring systems provide real-time alerts and notifications to operators or maintenance personnel when abnormal conditions or faults are detected. By providing timely warnings and actionable insights, AI systems enable proactive response and intervention, minimizing downtime and improving system reliability.

Overall, AI-driven fault detection and diagnosis systems play a critical role in ensuring the safety, reliability, and performance of railway operations by enabling early detection of faults, proactive maintenance strategies, and effective problem resolution. These systems enhance operational efficiency, reduce downtime, and improve the overall resilience of railway infrastructure and rolling stock.

ENHANCING PASSENGER SERVICES

AI-powered passenger services are transforming customer experiences in railway operations by providing personalized, efficient, and seamless travel experiences. Here are some key applications of AI in enhancing passenger services:

1. Personalized Recommendations and Assistance:

- AI algorithms analyze passenger data, including travel history, preferences, and demographics, to provide personalized recommendations for travel routes, services, and amenities. By understanding individual preferences and behaviors, AI-powered systems can offer tailored suggestions for dining options, entertainment, activities, and accommodations, enhancing the overall travel experience.

2. Real-time Travel Assistance:

- AI-powered virtual assistants and chatbots provide real-time assistance to passengers, offering information and guidance on travel-related inquiries, such as ticketing, schedules, delays, connections, and amenities. By leveraging natural language processing (NLP) and machine learning algorithms, virtual assistants can understand passenger queries, provide accurate responses, and offer personalized recommendations, improving customer satisfaction and reducing wait times.

3. Predictive Service Alerts:

- AI algorithms analyze real-time data from various sources, including sensors, weather forecasts, and operational systems, to predict potential service disruptions, delays, or cancellations. By proactively alerting passengers about upcoming changes or issues, AI-powered systems enable passengers to plan alternative routes, adjust schedules, or make contingency arrangements, minimizing inconvenience and frustration.

4. Smart Ticketing and Fare Management:

- AI-powered ticketing systems optimize fare pricing, promotions, and discounts based on demand forecasts, passenger profiles, and market trends. By analyzing historical booking data, purchasing patterns, and pricing strategies, AI algorithms can dynamically adjust ticket prices and offerings to maximize revenue while ensuring affordability and accessibility for passengers.

5. Automated Language Translation:

- AI-powered translation services enable multilingual communication between passengers and railway staff, facilitating seamless interactions and addressing language barriers. By leveraging speech recognition and machine translation technologies, AI systems can translate announcements, signage, instructions, and inquiries in real-time, enhancing accessibility and inclusivity for passengers from diverse linguistic backgrounds.

6. Intelligent Crowd Management:

- AI-based crowd management systems analyze passenger flow patterns, congestion levels, and queue lengths to optimize station layouts, staffing levels, and crowd control measures. By dynamically adjusting signage, barriers, and personnel deployment, AI systems can mitigate overcrowding, reduce wait times, and improve the overall flow of passengers through stations and terminals.

7. Personalized Entertainment and Information Services:

- AI-powered entertainment and information services offer personalized content, including news, weather updates, entertainment recommendations, and destination guides, tailored to passengers' preferences and interests. By leveraging data analytics and content curation algorithms, AI systems can deliver relevant and engaging content to passengers during their journey, enhancing comfort and satisfaction.

8. Feedback Analysis and Service Improvement:
  - AI algorithms analyze passenger feedback, reviews, and social media posts to identify trends, patterns, and areas for improvement in service delivery. By aggregating and analyzing sentiment data, AI-powered systems provide actionable insights to railway operators, enabling them to address issues, implement enhancements, and continuously improve the passenger experience.

Overall, AI-powered passenger services offer significant opportunities for railway operators to enhance customer experiences, improve service quality, and differentiate themselves in a competitive market. By leveraging AI technologies, railway operators can deliver personalized, efficient, and enjoyable travel experiences that meet the evolving needs and expectations of passengers.

ENHANCING TICKETING AND RESERVATION SYSTEMS

AI-powered ticketing and reservation systems are revolutionizing the passenger experience in railway operations by offering streamlined booking processes, personalized recommendations, and efficient management of ticketing services. Here are some key applications of AI in enhancing ticketing and reservation systems for railway passengers:

1. Dynamic Pricing and Fare Optimization:

- AI algorithms analyze historical booking data, demand forecasts, and market trends to optimize ticket pricing and fare structures dynamically. By adjusting ticket prices based on factors such as demand, time of booking, seat availability, and competitor pricing, AI-powered systems maximize revenue while ensuring competitiveness and affordability for passengers.

2. Personalized Ticket Recommendations:

- AI-powered recommendation engines analyze passenger profiles, preferences, and travel history to offer personalized ticket recommendations tailored to individual preferences and requirements. By understanding passenger preferences for factors such as travel dates, times, routes, seating preferences, and amenities, AI systems can suggest the most suitable ticket options, enhancing the booking experience and increasing customer satisfaction.

3. Predictive Seat Allocation and Availability Forecasting:

- AI algorithms predict seat availability and occupancy levels on trains based on historical booking patterns, cancellations, and no-show rates. By forecasting seat availability in real-time, AI-powered systems enable passengers to make informed decisions when booking tickets and selecting preferred seating arrangements, reducing the risk of overbooking and maximizing seat utilization.

4. Intelligent Booking Assistance and Chatbots:

- AI-powered chatbots and virtual assistants provide real-time booking assistance to passengers, guiding them through the ticketing process, answering inquiries, and resolving issues efficiently. By leveraging natural language processing (NLP) and machine learning algorithms, chatbots can understand passenger queries, offer personalized recommendations, and facilitate seamless booking experiences, reducing wait times and enhancing customer satisfaction.

5. Automated Ticket Verification and Validation:

- AI-powered ticket validation systems automate the process of ticket verification and validation at station entrances and onboard trains using image recognition and machine learning algorithms. By analyzing ticket barcodes, QR codes, or biometric data, AI systems can verify ticket authenticity, validity, and entitlements quickly and accurately, improving security and reducing the risk of fare evasion.

6. Predictive Ticketing and Reservation Management:

- AI algorithms predict future ticket demand and reservation patterns based on historical data, seasonal trends, and event calendars. By anticipating peak travel periods, busy routes, and high-demand services, AI-powered systems enable railway operators to proactively manage ticket inventory, allocate resources, and optimize capacity to meet passenger demand effectively.

7. Automated Refund and Cancellation Processing:

- AI-powered refund and cancellation systems automate the process of handling refund requests and ticket cancellations, reducing manual intervention and processing times. By analyzing refund policies, ticket terms, and customer requests, AI systems can expedite refund processing, issue credits or vouchers, and provide notifications to passengers, improving efficiency and customer service.

8. Fraud Detection and Prevention:

- AI algorithms analyze transaction data, user behavior, and payment patterns to detect and prevent fraudulent activities, such as ticket fraud, identity theft, or payment fraud. By applying machine learning techniques, anomaly detection algorithms, and pattern recognition, AI-powered fraud detection systems can identify suspicious transactions, verify user identities, and mitigate risks effectively, safeguarding ticketing systems and ensuring integrity and security.

Overall, AI-powered ticketing and reservation systems offer significant benefits for railway passengers and operators, including improved convenience, personalization, efficiency, and security. By leveraging AI technologies, railway operators can optimize ticketing processes, enhance customer experiences, and drive revenue growth in a competitive market.

PERSONALIZED TRAVEL RECOMMENDATIONS

AI-powered passenger services for personalized travel recommendations leverage advanced algorithms and data analytics to offer tailored suggestions and itineraries that match individual preferences and needs. Here are some key applications of AI in providing personalized travel recommendations for railway passengers:

1. Travel Preference Analysis:
   - AI algorithms analyze passenger data, including travel history, booking preferences, demographic information, and feedback, to understand individual preferences and behavior patterns. By processing this data, AI systems can identify passengers' preferred travel destinations, routes, travel times, seating preferences, amenities, and other relevant factors.

2. Destination Discovery and Exploration:
   - AI-powered recommendation engines suggest personalized travel destinations, attractions, activities, and experiences based on passengers' interests, demographics, and past travel behavior. By analyzing factors such as destination popularity, user ratings, reviews, and social media activity, AI systems can recommend relevant and engaging travel experiences that match passengers' preferences and aspirations.

3. Route Optimization and Multi-modal Travel:

- AI algorithms optimize travel routes and itineraries based on passengers' preferences, constraints, and objectives. By considering factors such as travel time, cost, convenience, mode of transportation, and environmental impact, AI-powered systems can recommend the most efficient and personalized travel routes, including multi-modal options such as train, bus, metro, or ride-sharing services.

4. Personalized Accommodation and Dining Recommendations:
- AI-powered recommendation systems suggest personalized accommodation options, restaurants, cafes, and dining experiences that align with passengers' preferences and dietary restrictions. By analyzing factors such as location, price, cuisine, ambiance, and user reviews, AI systems can recommend suitable dining and lodging options that meet passengers' tastes and preferences.

5. Activity and Entertainment Suggestions:
- AI algorithms recommend personalized activities, events, tours, and entertainment options based on passengers' interests, preferences, and availability. By analyzing factors such as event calendars, user preferences, past attendance, and social media activity, AI-powered systems can suggest relevant and engaging activities and experiences that enhance passengers' travel experiences.

6. Real-time Travel Updates and Alerts:
- AI-powered recommendation engines provide real-time updates, alerts, and notifications to passengers about travel-related information, such as delays, cancellations, disruptions, or alternative routes. By leveraging real-time data feeds, predictive analytics, and user preferences, AI systems can deliver timely and relevant updates that help passengers stay informed and plan their journeys effectively.

7. Context-aware Recommendations:
- AI-powered recommendation systems provide context-

aware recommendations that consider passengers' current location, time of day, weather conditions, and nearby attractions or points of interest. By analyzing contextual information in real-time, AI systems can offer relevant and personalized recommendations that enhance passengers' travel experiences and satisfaction.

8. Continuous Learning and Adaptation:

- AI algorithms continuously learn from passenger interactions, feedback, and preferences to improve the accuracy and relevance of travel recommendations over time. By incorporating user feedback, updating preferences, and adapting to changing circumstances, AI-powered systems can deliver increasingly personalized and tailored recommendations that meet passengers' evolving needs and preferences.

Overall, AI-powered passenger services for personalized travel recommendations enhance the overall travel experience by providing tailored suggestions, optimizing travel itineraries, and facilitating seamless journey planning for railway passengers. By leveraging AI technologies, railway operators can differentiate their services, increase customer satisfaction, and foster loyalty in a competitive market.

PASSENGER SAFETY AND SECURITY

AI-powered passenger services for safety and security measures aim to enhance the security and well-being of railway passengers by leveraging advanced technologies and data analytics. Here are some key applications of AI in providing safety and security measures for passengers in railway operations:

1. Video Surveillance and Threat Detection:
   - AI algorithms analyze video feeds from surveillance cameras installed in stations, trains, and other railway facilities to detect suspicious behaviors, unauthorized access, or security threats. By applying computer vision techniques such as object detection, facial recognition, and anomaly detection, AI systems can identify potential security breaches or safety concerns and alert security personnel in real-time.

2. Crowd Monitoring and Management:
   - AI-powered crowd monitoring systems analyze video feeds and sensor data to monitor passenger flow, congestion levels, and crowd dynamics in stations and terminals. By identifying areas of overcrowding, bottlenecks, or safety hazards, AI systems can facilitate proactive crowd management measures, such as rerouting passengers, deploying additional staff, or adjusting security protocols to ensure passenger safety and security.

3. Biometric Authentication and Access Control:
   - AI-based biometric authentication systems verify

passengers' identities using facial recognition, fingerprint scans, or iris recognition technologies. By securely authenticating passengers' identities, AI systems can prevent unauthorized access, deter criminal activities, and enhance the overall security of railway facilities and services.

4. Emergency Response and Incident Management:

- AI-powered incident management systems analyze real-time data from sensors, communication networks, and surveillance systems to detect emergencies, such as fires, accidents, or security incidents. By automatically detecting and classifying incidents, AI systems can trigger emergency response protocols, notify relevant authorities, and coordinate rescue and evacuation efforts to ensure passenger safety and minimize the impact of emergencies.

5. Predictive Maintenance for Safety Equipment:

- AI algorithms analyze sensor data from safety equipment, such as fire detection systems, emergency brakes, and evacuation systems, to predict potential failures or malfunctions. By proactively identifying maintenance needs and addressing safety equipment issues, AI-powered systems ensure the reliability and effectiveness of safety measures, reducing the risk of accidents or incidents affecting passengers.

6. Real-time Communication and Alerts:

- AI-powered communication systems provide real-time alerts, notifications, and updates to passengers about safety-related information, such as emergency procedures, evacuation routes, security advisories, or travel advisories. By delivering timely and actionable information, AI systems empower passengers to make informed decisions and respond effectively to safety and security threats.

7. Behavioral Analytics and Risk Assessment:

- AI algorithms analyze passenger behavior, travel patterns, and interactions to assess security risks and detect abnormal or suspicious behaviors. By monitoring passenger activity in real-time and correlating it with historical data, AI systems can identify potential security threats, such as unauthorized access, suspicious packages, or disruptive behavior, and alert security personnel to take appropriate action.

8. Integration with Law Enforcement and Emergency Services:
   - AI-powered safety and security systems integrate with law enforcement agencies, emergency services, and first responders to facilitate coordinated responses to security incidents or emergencies. By providing real-time situational awareness, actionable intelligence, and interoperable communication channels, AI systems enable effective collaboration and coordination among stakeholders to mitigate risks and ensure passenger safety and security.

Overall, AI-powered passenger services for safety and security measures play a crucial role in protecting passengers, staff, and assets in railway operations. By leveraging advanced technologies and data analytics, railway operators can enhance security protocols, improve emergency response capabilities, and foster a safe and secure environment for passengers to travel and commute.

FREIGHT SCHEDULING AND ROUTING

AI in freight operations revolutionizes freight scheduling and routing by optimizing routes, reducing transit times, and enhancing operational efficiency. Here are some key applications of AI in freight scheduling and routing:

1. Dynamic Routing Optimization:
   - AI algorithms analyze real-time data, such as traffic conditions, weather forecasts, and delivery constraints, to dynamically optimize freight routes. By considering factors such as distance, fuel efficiency, road conditions, and delivery deadlines, AI systems can generate optimal routing plans that minimize transit times, reduce fuel consumption, and maximize delivery efficiency.

2. Predictive Analytics for Demand Forecasting:
   - AI-powered demand forecasting models analyze historical data, market trends, and customer behavior to predict future freight demand accurately. By forecasting shipment volumes, delivery patterns, and peak demand periods, AI systems enable freight operators to anticipate capacity requirements, plan resources, and optimize scheduling to meet customer needs effectively.

3. Real-time Traffic Management:
   - AI algorithms monitor traffic conditions and congestion levels in real-time using data from GPS sensors, traffic cameras, and navigation systems. By analyzing traffic patterns, bottlenecks, and alternative routes, AI systems can dynamically

reroute freight vehicles to avoid delays, minimize congestion, and optimize delivery schedules.

4. Load Balancing and Capacity Optimization:
- AI-powered load balancing algorithms optimize the allocation of freight loads across vehicles, routes, and delivery schedules to maximize capacity utilization and minimize empty miles. By analyzing factors such as load sizes, vehicle capacities, and delivery priorities, AI systems can match freight shipments with available capacity and optimize scheduling to minimize costs and improve efficiency.

5. Multi-modal Routing and Intermodal Transportation:
- AI algorithms optimize freight routing across multiple modes of transportation, including trucks, trains, ships, and planes, to leverage the strengths of each mode and minimize transit times and costs. By considering factors such as distance, transit times, transportation costs, and modal constraints, AI systems can identify the most efficient and cost-effective routing options for freight shipments.

6. Predictive Maintenance for Fleet Management:
- AI-powered predictive maintenance systems analyze sensor data from freight vehicles to predict potential equipment failures or maintenance needs. By forecasting maintenance requirements, downtime, and repair costs, AI systems enable fleet operators to schedule maintenance proactively, minimize disruptions, and optimize vehicle availability for freight scheduling and routing.

7. Optimized Last-mile Delivery:
- AI algorithms optimize last-mile delivery routes and schedules to maximize efficiency and minimize delivery costs. By considering factors such as delivery locations, time windows, traffic conditions, and delivery priorities, AI systems can generate optimized routing plans that minimize delivery times, reduce fuel consumption, and improve customer satisfaction.

8. Continuous Learning and Adaptation:

- AI-powered freight scheduling and routing systems continuously learn from historical data, operational feedback, and external factors to improve routing algorithms and decision-making processes over time. By incorporating feedback from freight operations, customer preferences, and market dynamics, AI systems can adapt to changing conditions, optimize routing strategies, and enhance overall performance.

Overall, AI in freight operations for scheduling and routing offers significant opportunities for improving efficiency, reducing costs, and enhancing customer satisfaction. By leveraging advanced algorithms and data analytics, freight operators can optimize routing plans, minimize transit times, and streamline operations to meet the growing demands of the global supply chain.

CARGO TRACKING AND MONITORING

AI in freight operations transforms cargo tracking and monitoring by providing real-time visibility, predictive analytics, and proactive management of cargo shipments. Here are some key applications of AI in cargo tracking and monitoring:

1. Real-time Tracking and Tracing:
   - AI-powered tracking systems use GPS, RFID, and IoT sensors to monitor the location and status of cargo shipments in real-time. By collecting and analyzing data from these sensors, AI systems provide accurate and up-to-date information about the whereabouts of cargo, enabling shippers and logistics providers to track shipments throughout the supply chain.

2. Predictive Analytics for Shipment Delays:
   - AI algorithms analyze historical shipment data, traffic patterns, weather forecasts, and other relevant factors to predict potential delays or disruptions in cargo shipments. By forecasting delivery times, transit routes, and potential bottlenecks, AI systems enable shippers to proactively manage risks, adjust schedules, and mitigate the impact of delays on supply chain operations.

3. Route Optimization and Dynamic Routing:
   - AI-powered route optimization algorithms analyze real-time data on traffic conditions, road closures, and delivery constraints to dynamically adjust shipment routes and

schedules. By considering factors such as distance, travel time, fuel efficiency, and delivery priorities, AI systems optimize routing plans to minimize transit times, reduce costs, and improve on-time delivery performance.

4. Cargo Security and Tamper Detection:
   - AI-based security systems analyze sensor data and video feeds to detect unauthorized access, tampering, or theft of cargo shipments. By monitoring cargo containers, vehicles, and storage facilities in real-time, AI systems can identify suspicious activities, trigger alerts, and notify security personnel to take immediate action to safeguard the integrity and security of cargo shipments.

5. Condition Monitoring and Quality Control:
   - AI algorithms analyze sensor data from IoT devices to monitor environmental conditions, such as temperature, humidity, and pressure, inside cargo containers or storage facilities. By continuously monitoring these parameters, AI systems can detect deviations from acceptable ranges, identify potential risks to cargo quality, and trigger corrective actions to prevent spoilage or damage to sensitive goods.

6. Supply Chain Visibility and Collaboration:
   - AI-powered supply chain visibility platforms provide end-to-end visibility into cargo shipments, enabling stakeholders across the supply chain to collaborate and coordinate activities more effectively. By sharing real-time information on shipment status, location, and ETA, AI systems facilitate proactive decision-making, improve communication, and enhance collaboration among shippers, carriers, suppliers, and customers.

7. Predictive Maintenance for Transport Equipment:
   - AI algorithms analyze sensor data from transportation equipment, such as trucks, ships, and aircraft, to predict potential equipment failures or maintenance needs. By

forecasting maintenance requirements, downtime, and repair costs, AI systems enable fleet operators to schedule maintenance proactively, minimize disruptions, and ensure the reliability and availability of transport assets for cargo shipments.

8. Customer Service and Transparency:

- AI-powered cargo tracking systems provide customers with real-time updates, notifications, and alerts about their shipments' status and location. By offering self-service tracking tools, mobile apps, and personalized notifications, AI systems enhance customer satisfaction, transparency, and trust by keeping customers informed and engaged throughout the shipping process.

Overall, AI in freight operations for cargo tracking and monitoring offers significant benefits for shippers, logistics providers, and customers by providing real-time visibility, predictive insights, and proactive management of cargo shipments. By leveraging advanced algorithms and data analytics, freight operators can optimize supply chain performance, reduce risks, and enhance customer experiences in the increasingly complex and dynamic world of global logistics.

OPTIMIZING FREIGHT LOGISTICS

AI in freight operations optimizes freight logistics by leveraging advanced algorithms and data analytics to streamline processes, reduce costs, and improve efficiency across the supply chain. Here are some key applications of AI in optimizing freight logistics:

1. Route Optimization:
   - AI algorithms analyze various factors such as distance, traffic conditions, delivery schedules, and fuel costs to optimize freight routes. By considering dynamic variables and constraints, AI systems can generate the most efficient routes that minimize transportation costs, reduce transit times, and improve on-time delivery performance.

2. Load Planning and Optimization:
   - AI-powered load planning algorithms optimize the allocation of cargo across transportation assets such as trucks, ships, and containers. By considering factors such as cargo volumes, weight capacities, and delivery priorities, AI systems maximize load utilization, minimize empty miles, and reduce transportation costs.

3. Multi-modal Transportation Planning:
   - AI algorithms optimize freight logistics by incorporating multiple modes of transportation, such as trucks, trains, ships, and planes, into the transportation network. By analyzing factors such as transit times, costs, and capacity constraints for each mode, AI systems identify the most efficient and cost-

effective transportation options for freight shipments.

4. Inventory Management and Stock Optimization:

- AI-powered inventory management systems analyze historical sales data, demand forecasts, and supply chain constraints to optimize inventory levels and stock allocation. By balancing inventory levels with demand variability, lead times, and storage costs, AI systems minimize stockouts, reduce excess inventory, and improve inventory turnover rates.

5. Warehouse Automation and Robotics:

- AI-driven warehouse automation systems optimize freight logistics by automating warehouse operations such as picking, packing, and sorting. By deploying robotic systems equipped with AI algorithms, warehouses can increase efficiency, reduce labor costs, and improve order fulfillment accuracy, leading to faster throughput and better customer service.

6. Predictive Maintenance for Transportation Equipment:

- AI algorithms analyze sensor data from transportation assets such as trucks, ships, and planes to predict potential equipment failures or maintenance needs. By forecasting maintenance requirements, downtime, and repair costs, AI systems enable fleet operators to schedule maintenance proactively, minimize disruptions, and ensure the reliability and availability of transportation equipment for freight logistics.

7. Dynamic Capacity Management:

- AI-powered capacity management systems dynamically adjust transportation capacity based on demand forecasts, seasonal trends, and market conditions. By optimizing capacity allocation and pricing strategies, AI systems enable transportation providers to maximize revenue, minimize costs, and maintain service levels in response to changing demand patterns.

8. Supply Chain Visibility and Collaboration:

- AI-powered supply chain visibility platforms provide end-to-end visibility into freight logistics operations, enabling stakeholders to collaborate and coordinate activities more effectively. By sharing real-time information on shipment status, location, and ETA, AI systems facilitate proactive decision-making, improve communication, and enhance collaboration among shippers, carriers, suppliers, and customers.

Overall, AI in freight operations optimizes logistics processes, improves decision-making, and enhances efficiency across the supply chain. By leveraging advanced algorithms and data analytics, freight operators can reduce costs, minimize risks, and deliver superior service to customers in the increasingly competitive and dynamic world of global logistics.

AI IN WAREHOUSE MANAGEMENT

AI in freight operations revolutionizes warehouse management by automating processes, optimizing workflows, and improving efficiency across various warehouse operations. Here are some key applications of AI in warehouse management:

1. Inventory Optimization:
   - AI algorithms analyze historical sales data, demand forecasts, and supply chain trends to optimize inventory levels. By dynamically adjusting stock levels based on demand variability, lead times, and storage costs, AI systems minimize stockouts, reduce excess inventory, and improve inventory turnover rates.

2. Warehouse Layout Optimization:
   - AI-powered warehouse layout optimization algorithms analyze factors such as SKU volumes, picking frequencies, and storage requirements to design efficient warehouse layouts. By optimizing the placement of inventory, aisles, and storage racks, AI systems minimize travel distances, reduce labor costs, and improve throughput in the warehouse.

3. Automated Order Picking and Fulfillment:
   - AI-driven robotic systems automate order picking, packing, and fulfillment processes in warehouses. By deploying robots equipped with AI algorithms, warehouses can increase picking accuracy, reduce fulfillment times, and improve overall productivity, leading to faster order processing and better customer service.

4. Predictive Maintenance for Equipment:

- AI algorithms analyze sensor data from warehouse equipment, such as conveyor belts, forklifts, and automated guided vehicles (AGVs), to predict potential equipment failures or maintenance needs. By forecasting maintenance requirements, downtime, and repair costs, AI systems enable warehouse operators to schedule maintenance proactively, minimize disruptions, and ensure the reliability of warehouse operations.

5. Dynamic Slotting Optimization:

- AI-powered slotting optimization algorithms optimize the allocation of inventory to storage locations based on factors such as SKU characteristics, demand patterns, and picking frequencies. By continuously analyzing SKU movement and order profiles, AI systems ensure that fast-moving items are placed in easily accessible locations, minimizing travel times and improving picking efficiency.

6. Task Allocation and Workforce Management:

- AI algorithms optimize task allocation and workforce management in warehouses by considering factors such as order priorities, employee skills, and equipment availability. By dynamically assigning tasks to workers and coordinating workflows, AI systems maximize labor productivity, reduce idle time, and improve overall operational efficiency.

7. Quality Control and Defect Detection:

- AI-powered vision systems inspect incoming inventory for defects, damages, or discrepancies using machine vision algorithms. By analyzing images captured by cameras, AI systems can detect defects such as mislabeled products, damaged packaging, or missing items, enabling warehouse operators to take corrective action and maintain product quality standards.

8. Real-time Performance Monitoring and Optimization:

- AI-powered warehouse management systems provide real-time monitoring of key performance indicators (KPIs) such as order fulfillment rates, inventory accuracy, and labor productivity. By analyzing performance data in real-time, AI systems identify bottlenecks, inefficiencies, and opportunities for improvement, enabling warehouse operators to make data-driven decisions and optimize operations continuously.

Overall, AI in warehouse management streamlines processes, enhances productivity, and improves accuracy in freight operations. By leveraging advanced algorithms and automation technologies, warehouses can optimize workflows, reduce costs, and deliver superior service to customers in the dynamic and competitive logistics industry.

ADVANCED AI TECHNIQUES

In rail transportation, machine learning algorithms are utilized for predictive analytics to forecast various factors such as equipment failures, maintenance needs, passenger demand, and operational performance. Here are some advanced AI techniques in rail transportation predictive analytics:

1. Predictive Maintenance:
   - Machine learning algorithms analyze historical maintenance records, sensor data, and equipment telemetry to predict potential failures or degradation in rail infrastructure and rolling stock. Techniques such as regression analysis, time-series forecasting, and anomaly detection are employed to identify patterns indicative of impending failures, enabling proactive maintenance interventions to minimize downtime and improve reliability.

2. Fault Detection and Diagnosis:
   - Machine learning models are trained on sensor data from railway equipment and infrastructure to detect anomalies and diagnose faults in real-time. Supervised learning techniques such as classification and anomaly detection algorithms are used to differentiate between normal and abnormal operating conditions, identifying potential issues such as track defects, signal failures, or rolling stock malfunctions before they escalate into critical failures.

3. Demand Forecasting:

- Machine learning algorithms analyze historical passenger data, ticket sales, and external factors such as weather, events, and holidays to forecast passenger demand for rail services. Time-series forecasting models, regression analysis, and ensemble methods are employed to predict future ridership levels, enabling railway operators to optimize service levels, allocate resources efficiently, and plan capacity to meet passenger needs.

4. Traffic Flow Prediction:

- Machine learning techniques are applied to analyze historical traffic patterns, train schedules, and infrastructure capacity to predict future traffic flows on railway networks. Models such as recurrent neural networks (RNNs), convolutional neural networks (CNNs), and graph-based algorithms are used to forecast congestion levels, identify potential bottlenecks, and optimize train schedules to improve network efficiency and reliability.

5. Energy Consumption Optimization:

- Machine learning algorithms analyze data from onboard sensors, weather forecasts, and operational parameters to optimize energy consumption in rail operations. Regression models, reinforcement learning algorithms, and optimization techniques are employed to identify energy-saving opportunities, optimize train speeds, and minimize energy costs while maintaining schedule adherence and service quality.

6. Predictive Delay Management:

- Machine learning models are trained on historical delay data, incident reports, and external factors such as weather conditions and infrastructure maintenance schedules to predict potential delays in rail operations. Classification algorithms, time-series analysis, and ensemble methods are utilized to forecast delay probabilities, enabling railway operators to implement proactive measures such as schedule adjustments, route diversions, and resource reallocation to mitigate the impact of delays on service reliability.

7. Customer Behavior Prediction:

- Machine learning algorithms analyze passenger behavior data, booking patterns, and feedback to predict customer preferences, satisfaction levels, and future travel intentions. Classification models, clustering techniques, and sentiment analysis algorithms are employed to segment passengers, personalize services, and tailor marketing strategies to enhance customer experience and loyalty.

8. Dynamic Pricing and Revenue Optimization:

- Machine learning algorithms analyze historical booking data, demand patterns, and market dynamics to optimize ticket pricing and revenue management strategies. Pricing models, demand forecasting techniques, and optimization algorithms are used to dynamically adjust ticket prices, allocate inventory, and maximize revenue while balancing factors such as yield, load factors, and customer segmentation.

Overall, machine learning algorithms play a critical role in predictive analytics for rail transportation, enabling railway operators to anticipate future events, optimize resource allocation, and enhance operational efficiency to meet the evolving needs of passengers and stakeholders in the railway industry.

DEEP LEARNING APPLICATIONS

In rail transportation, deep learning applications in image recognition for railway safety play a crucial role in identifying potential hazards, monitoring infrastructure integrity, and ensuring passenger and employee safety. Here are some advanced AI techniques using deep learning for image recognition in railway safety:

1. Track Inspection and Maintenance:
   - Deep learning models are trained on large datasets of images captured by trackside cameras or drones to detect anomalies, defects, and damage on railway tracks. Convolutional neural networks (CNNs) and deep learning architectures such as YOLO (You Only Look Once) are employed to recognize track irregularities such as cracks, fractures, or misalignments, enabling early detection and proactive maintenance to prevent accidents and service disruptions.

2. Object Detection and Classification:
   - Deep learning algorithms are utilized to detect and classify objects of interest near railway tracks, including trespassers, vehicles, wildlife, and debris. CNNs and object detection frameworks such as Faster R-CNN (Region-based Convolutional Neural Network) are trained to recognize and categorize objects in real-time, enabling railway operators to identify potential safety hazards, trigger alerts, and take appropriate actions to mitigate risks and ensure safety.

3. Level Crossing Monitoring:
- Deep learning models analyze images from surveillance cameras installed at level crossings to detect vehicles, pedestrians, and other obstacles on railway tracks. CNNs and recurrent neural networks (RNNs) are employed to identify crossing violations, track vehicle movements, and predict potential collisions, enabling automated warning systems to alert train operators and motorists, preventing accidents and improving level crossing safety.

4. Signal and Sign Recognition:
- Deep learning algorithms are trained to recognize railway signals, signs, and markers from images captured by onboard cameras or trackside sensors. CNNs and image recognition techniques such as semantic segmentation are used to interpret visual cues and infer signal states, trackside warnings, and track conditions, enabling automated systems to monitor signal integrity, detect anomalies, and ensure compliance with safety regulations.

5. Platform Safety Monitoring:
- Deep learning models analyze surveillance footage from platform cameras to monitor passenger behavior, detect overcrowding, and identify potential security threats. CNNs and video analytics algorithms are trained to recognize suspicious activities, abandoned objects, or unauthorized access, enabling security personnel to respond promptly, ensure crowd control, and maintain a safe environment for passengers and staff.

6. Worker Safety and Asset Protection:
- Deep learning algorithms analyze images from onboard cameras or wearable devices to monitor worker activities, identify safety violations, and prevent accidents in railway yards and maintenance facilities. CNNs and human activity recognition models are employed to detect hazardous behaviors, such as unauthorized access to restricted areas, unsafe working

practices, or equipment malfunctions, enabling supervisors to intervene and enforce safety protocols.

7. Infrastructure Monitoring and Inspection:
   - Deep learning techniques are applied to analyze images captured by drones or inspection vehicles to assess the condition of railway infrastructure, including bridges, tunnels, and embankments. CNNs and semantic segmentation algorithms are trained to identify structural defects, erosion, or deterioration, enabling engineers to prioritize maintenance tasks, allocate resources efficiently, and ensure the structural integrity and safety of railway assets.

8. Emergency Response and Incident Management:
   - Deep learning models analyze real-time images from onboard cameras or emergency response drones to assess the severity of accidents, incidents, or natural disasters on railway tracks. CNNs and object detection algorithms are used to identify casualties, assess damage, and prioritize rescue efforts, enabling emergency responders to coordinate interventions, allocate resources effectively, and minimize the impact of emergencies on railway safety.

Overall, deep learning applications in image recognition for railway safety enhance situational awareness, enable proactive risk mitigation, and improve safety outcomes in rail transportation. By leveraging advanced AI techniques, railway operators can detect potential hazards, monitor infrastructure integrity, and ensure a safe and secure environment for passengers, employees, and communities along railway networks.

NATURAL LANGUAGE PROCESSING

In rail transportation, natural language processing (NLP) is increasingly being used for customer service automation to enhance passenger experiences, streamline communication, and improve operational efficiency. Here are some advanced AI techniques using NLP for customer service automation in rail transportation:

1. Automated Ticketing and Reservation Systems:
  - NLP-powered chatbots and virtual assistants enable passengers to book tickets, check train schedules, and make reservations using natural language commands and queries. By leveraging NLP techniques such as intent recognition, entity extraction, and dialogue management, chatbots can understand passenger requests, provide personalized recommendations, and facilitate seamless booking experiences, reducing reliance on manual ticketing processes and improving customer satisfaction.

2. Real-time Passenger Assistance:
  - NLP-based chatbots and virtual assistants provide real-time assistance to passengers during their journey, answering inquiries, providing travel information, and addressing service-related issues. By analyzing passenger queries, sentiment, and intent, NLP systems can deliver relevant and timely responses, offer alternative travel options, and resolve customer concerns efficiently, enhancing the overall travel experience and fostering passenger loyalty.

3. Automated Information Retrieval:

- NLP algorithms parse and analyze textual information from various sources, such as websites, social media, and service announcements, to extract relevant travel updates, service alerts, and safety advisories for passengers. By processing unstructured data and applying information retrieval techniques, NLP systems can curate and summarize relevant information, deliver personalized notifications, and keep passengers informed about disruptions, delays, or changes in service status.

4. Voice-enabled Ticketing and Inquiry Systems:

- NLP-powered voice recognition systems enable passengers to interact with ticketing and inquiry systems using natural language voice commands. By integrating voice recognition technology with NLP algorithms, railway operators can offer hands-free access to ticketing services, reservation inquiries, and travel information, allowing passengers to access services and information conveniently, especially while on the move or without access to traditional interfaces.

5. Sentiment Analysis and Customer Feedback:

- NLP techniques such as sentiment analysis are used to analyze passenger feedback, reviews, and social media conversations to assess customer satisfaction levels and identify areas for improvement in rail services. By analyzing textual data from customer reviews, surveys, and social media posts, NLP systems can extract sentiment polarity, identify emerging issues, and prioritize action plans to address passenger concerns, improving service quality and reputation management.

6. Multilingual Support and Translation Services:

- NLP algorithms enable railway operators to offer multilingual support and translation services to passengers speaking different languages. By employing machine translation models and language understanding techniques, NLP systems can translate inquiries, announcements, and service information into multiple languages, catering to the diverse linguistic needs of passengers and facilitating communication across language barriers.

7. Contextual Understanding and Dialogue Management:

- NLP-powered chatbots and virtual assistants utilize contextual understanding and dialogue management techniques to maintain coherent and engaging conversations with passengers. By tracking conversation history, maintaining context, and generating relevant responses, NLP systems can provide personalized assistance, anticipate passenger needs, and guide users through complex inquiries or transactions, enhancing the overall conversational experience.

8. Integration with Backend Systems and Knowledge Bases:

- NLP-based customer service automation systems integrate with backend databases, knowledge bases, and service management platforms to access and retrieve relevant information for passengers. By connecting to internal systems such as ticketing databases, train schedules, and service catalogs, NLP systems can provide accurate and up-to-date information, process transactions, and execute service requests seamlessly, improving efficiency and reducing response times.

Overall, NLP for customer service automation in rail transportation offers significant benefits in terms of efficiency, convenience, and customer satisfaction. By leveraging advanced AI techniques, railway operators can automate routine inquiries, personalize interactions, and deliver enhanced passenger experiences, contributing to the overall success and competitiveness of rail services in the modern era of transportation.

REINFORCEMENT LEARNING

Reinforcement learning (RL) is an advanced AI technique increasingly applied in rail transportation for train control optimization. RL enables autonomous decision-making by allowing systems to learn optimal control policies through trial and error interactions with the environment. Here's how RL can be applied for train control optimization:

1. Automated Train Dispatching:
   - RL algorithms can learn optimal dispatching strategies to manage train movements efficiently, considering factors such as network congestion, scheduling conflicts, and resource utilization. Agents are trained to make decisions in real-time to minimize delays, maximize throughput, and optimize resource allocation across the railway network.

2. Traffic Management and Scheduling:
   - RL techniques can optimize train schedules and traffic flow by learning dynamic dispatching policies that adapt to changing demand, disruptions, and network conditions. Agents learn to make decisions on train speeds, routes, and stops to minimize congestion, reduce energy consumption, and improve on-time performance across the railway network.

3. Energy-Efficient Train Operation:
   - RL algorithms can optimize train operation for energy efficiency by learning adaptive control policies that balance speed, acceleration, and braking to minimize energy

consumption while maintaining schedule adherence. Agents learn to adjust train behavior based on real-time feedback from sensors, optimizing energy usage across different operating conditions and terrain profiles.

4. Collision Avoidance and Safety:

- RL techniques can train agents to navigate railway networks safely and avoid collisions by learning predictive control policies that anticipate potential hazards and take proactive measures to mitigate risks. Agents learn to optimize train trajectories, braking distances, and speed profiles to ensure safe operations and comply with signaling rules and safety regulations.

5. Adaptive Control for Dynamic Environments:

- RL algorithms enable adaptive control in dynamic railway environments by learning policies that can generalize across different operating conditions, traffic patterns, and weather conditions. Agents learn to adapt their behavior based on environmental feedback and historical data, optimizing train operations for efficiency, reliability, and safety under varying circumstances.

6. Optimization of Junctions and Intersections:

- RL techniques can optimize train movements at junctions and intersections by learning decentralized control policies that coordinate train movements efficiently to minimize conflicts and maximize throughput. Agents learn to make decisions collaboratively, negotiating priority and sharing resources to optimize the flow of trains through complex railway networks.

7. Learning from Simulation and Virtual Environments:

- RL algorithms can leverage simulation environments to train control policies in virtual railway networks, enabling agents to explore and learn optimal strategies without risk to real-world operations. Agents learn from simulated interactions with the environment, gradually improving their performance through reinforcement learning and experience replay techniques.

8. Continuous Learning and Adaptation:

- RL systems can continuously learn and adapt to evolving railway conditions by updating control policies based on real-time data and feedback from the environment. Agents learn from operational experience, incorporating new information and adjusting their behavior to optimize train control in response to changing demand, infrastructure conditions, and operational constraints.

Overall, reinforcement learning for train control optimization offers significant potential to improve efficiency, safety, and reliability in rail transportation. By leveraging advanced AI techniques, railway operators can develop autonomous control systems that optimize train operations, reduce costs, and enhance the overall performance of railway networks in the face of increasing demands and complexities.

AI WITH IOT & BIG DATA ANALYTICS BY SENSOR NETWORKS

The integration of AI with IoT (Internet of Things) and Big Data analytics in railway sensor networks offers tremendous potential to enhance safety, efficiency, and reliability in railway systems. Here's how these technologies work together in railway sensor networks:

1. Data Collection with IoT Sensors:

- IoT sensors are deployed throughout railway systems to collect real-time data on various parameters such as train locations, speeds, temperatures, vibrations, track conditions, and environmental factors. These sensors continuously monitor the operational status of trains, tracks, signals, and infrastructure components, generating vast amounts of sensor data that capture the dynamics of railway operations.

2. Data Transmission and Connectivity:

- IoT devices in railway sensor networks are interconnected through wireless communication technologies such as Wi-Fi, cellular networks, or dedicated communication protocols like GSM-R (Global System for Mobile Communications – Railway). These networks facilitate seamless data transmission and connectivity between sensors, onboard systems, control centers, and backend analytics platforms, enabling real-time monitoring and control of railway assets.

3. Big Data Analytics for Real-time Insights:

- Big Data analytics platforms process and analyze the massive volumes of data generated by IoT sensors in railway systems. Advanced analytics techniques such as stream processing, complex event processing (CEP), and machine learning are applied to extract real-time insights, detect patterns, and identify anomalies in sensor data, enabling proactive decision-making and timely interventions to optimize railway operations.

4. Predictive Maintenance and Asset Management:

- AI-powered predictive maintenance models analyze sensor data from railway assets to predict potential failures, prioritize maintenance activities, and optimize asset lifecycle management. By applying machine learning algorithms to historical sensor data, predictive maintenance systems can forecast equipment degradation, schedule maintenance tasks, and prevent costly disruptions, enhancing the reliability and availability of railway infrastructure.

5. Real-time Monitoring and Control:

- AI algorithms process sensor data in real-time to monitor the operational status of trains, tracks, and infrastructure components, detecting abnormalities and triggering automated responses to maintain safety and efficiency. For example, AI-based control systems can adjust train speeds, switch settings, or signal configurations based on real-time sensor feedback, optimizing traffic flow and minimizing delays in railway operations.

6. Environmental Monitoring and Sustainability:

- IoT sensors collect environmental data such as air quality, noise levels, and emissions in railway systems, enabling operators to monitor environmental impacts and comply with regulatory requirements. Big Data analytics platforms analyze sensor data to assess environmental performance, identify areas for improvement, and develop strategies for enhancing sustainability and reducing environmental footprint in rail transportation.

7. Passenger Safety and Security:

- IoT sensors deployed in railway stations and trains monitor passenger movements, crowd densities, and security incidents to ensure passenger safety and security. Big Data analytics platforms process sensor data to detect anomalies, identify potential security threats, and coordinate emergency responses in real-time, enhancing situational awareness and improving incident management in railway operations.

8. Optimization of Traffic Flow and Capacity:

- AI algorithms analyze sensor data from railway networks to optimize traffic flow, capacity utilization, and scheduling of trains. By applying optimization techniques such as reinforcement learning and evolutionary algorithms, AI systems can dynamically adjust train schedules, route assignments, and signaling strategies to minimize congestion, maximize throughput, and improve overall efficiency in railway operations.

Overall, the integration of AI with IoT and Big Data analytics in railway sensor networks enables railway operators to leverage real-time data insights, predictive capabilities, and automated control mechanisms to optimize safety, efficiency, and reliability across the entire rail transportation ecosystem. By harnessing the power of these advanced technologies, railways can adapt to evolving demands, enhance passenger experiences, and drive innovation in the digital age of transportation.

DATA COLLECTION AND PROCESSING TECHNIQUE

The integration of AI with IoT and Big Data in railways involves sophisticated data collection and processing techniques to harness the vast amounts of sensor data generated by IoT devices. Here are some key data collection and processing techniques used in this integration:

1. Sensor Deployment and Instrumentation:
   - Railway systems are equipped with various IoT sensors strategically deployed across trains, tracks, signals, stations, and other infrastructure components. These sensors collect data on parameters such as train speed, location, acceleration, braking, track conditions, temperature, vibration, and environmental factors. Sensor types include accelerometers, GPS receivers, temperature sensors, pressure sensors, strain gauges, cameras, and environmental sensors.

2. Data Transmission and Connectivity:
   - IoT devices in railway systems are connected through wireless communication technologies such as Wi-Fi, cellular networks, Zigbee, LoRaWAN, or dedicated railway communication protocols like GSM-R. These networks facilitate seamless data transmission and connectivity between sensors, onboard systems, control centers, and backend analytics platforms, enabling real-time monitoring and control of railway

assets.

3. Edge Computing and Fog Computing:

- Edge computing and fog computing technologies are employed to process and analyze sensor data closer to the data source, reducing latency and bandwidth requirements. Edge devices installed onboard trains or along the railway track preprocess sensor data locally, performing initial filtering, aggregation, or anomaly detection before transmitting relevant data to centralized servers or cloud-based analytics platforms for further analysis.

4. Data Aggregation and Fusion:

- Sensor data collected from multiple sources are aggregated and fused to create a unified view of the railway system. Data aggregation techniques consolidate raw sensor data from distributed sensors into coherent datasets, while data fusion methods combine information from different sensor modalities to extract meaningful insights and enrich the understanding of railway operations, infrastructure conditions, and performance metrics.

5. Stream Processing and Complex Event Processing (CEP):

- Stream processing and CEP platforms analyze real-time data streams from IoT sensors to detect patterns, correlations, and anomalies as events occur. These platforms apply continuous queries, pattern recognition algorithms, and temporal logic rules to process high-velocity data streams, identify relevant events, and trigger automated responses or alerts based on predefined rules and thresholds.

6. Batch Processing and Data Warehousing:

- Batch processing techniques are used to analyze historical sensor data stored in data warehouses or distributed databases. Big Data platforms such as Hadoop, Spark, or Apache Flink perform batch processing tasks such as data cleaning, transformation, aggregation, and statistical analysis on large volumes of sensor data to extract insights, generate reports, and support decision-making in railway operations.

7. Machine Learning and AI Algorithms:
   - Machine learning algorithms and AI techniques are applied to analyze sensor data and extract actionable insights for predictive maintenance, anomaly detection, optimization, and decision support in railway operations. Supervised learning, unsupervised learning, reinforcement learning, and deep learning algorithms are used to train predictive models, detect patterns, classify events, and make predictions based on historical sensor data.

8. Data Visualization and Human-Machine Interaction:
   - Data visualization tools and dashboards present sensor data in intuitive formats, such as charts, graphs, maps, or dashboards, to facilitate understanding and decision-making by railway operators, maintenance crews, and other stakeholders. Interactive visualization interfaces enable users to explore data, drill down into details, and interact with analytical models to gain insights and take appropriate actions in real-time.

By leveraging these data collection and processing techniques, railway operators can harness the power of AI, IoT, and Big Data analytics to optimize safety, efficiency, and reliability in railway operations, ensuring smooth and reliable transportation services for passengers and freight alike.

REAL-TIME ANALYTICS

Real-time analytics for decision-making in railways, enabled by the integration of AI with IoT and Big Data technologies, facilitates proactive and data-driven responses to operational challenges. Here's how real-time analytics is leveraged for decision-making in railway systems:

1. Real-time Data Collection:
   - IoT sensors continuously collect data from various sources such as trains, tracks, signals, and stations in real-time. This data includes information on train locations, speeds, accelerations, braking, track conditions, environmental factors, and passenger flows.

2. Data Streaming and Processing:
   - Real-time data streams from IoT sensors are processed in-stream using technologies such as Apache Kafka, Apache Flink, or Apache Storm. These stream processing frameworks enable data ingestion, aggregation, filtering, and enrichment to transform raw sensor data into actionable insights in real-time.

3. Complex Event Processing (CEP):
   - CEP platforms analyze real-time data streams to detect patterns, correlations, and anomalies as events occur. By applying continuous queries, pattern recognition algorithms, and rules-based processing, CEP systems identify critical events and trigger automated responses or alerts based on predefined thresholds and business rules.

4. Predictive Analytics and Machine Learning:
   - Real-time analytics systems incorporate machine learning

models trained on historical data to make predictions and forecasts in real-time. These models include predictive maintenance algorithms, anomaly detection models, demand forecasting models, and optimization algorithms that continuously analyze streaming data to anticipate future events and optimize decision-making.

5. Dynamic Resource Allocation:
  - Real-time analytics systems optimize resource allocation by dynamically adjusting train schedules, crew assignments, and equipment deployments based on changing demand, disruptions, and resource availability. By analyzing real-time data on train movements, passenger flows, and infrastructure conditions, these systems optimize resource utilization and minimize operational costs while maintaining service levels.

6. Operational Monitoring and Control:
  - Real-time analytics platforms provide operators with live dashboards and visualization tools to monitor key performance indicators (KPIs), track operational metrics, and visualize data trends in real-time. Operators can monitor train performance, track incidents, and assess network congestion, enabling them to make informed decisions and take timely actions to address operational issues.

7. Automated Alerts and Notifications:
  - Real-time analytics systems generate automated alerts and notifications to alert operators to critical events or deviations from expected norms. These alerts can be sent via email, SMS, or push notifications to notify operators of incidents such as equipment failures, service disruptions, safety hazards, or security threats, enabling them to respond promptly and mitigate risks.

8. Continuous Improvement and Adaptation:
  - Real-time analytics systems continuously learn and adapt to changing conditions and operational feedback. Machine

learning algorithms analyze real-time data to update predictive models, optimize decision-making strategies, and improve system performance over time, ensuring that decision-making processes remain effective and adaptive in dynamic railway environments.

By leveraging real-time analytics for decision-making, railway operators can enhance operational efficiency, improve service reliability, and optimize resource utilization to deliver safe, reliable, and customer-centric transportation services in today's fast-paced and dynamic railway industry.

SUCCESS STORIES

Here are some case studies demonstrating successful implementations of AI with IoT and Big Data in railways:

1. Indian Railways - Predictive Maintenance:
   - Indian Railways collaborated with General Electric (GE) to implement a predictive maintenance solution using IoT sensors and Big Data analytics. Thousands of sensors were installed on locomotives and tracks to monitor equipment health and performance in real-time. Data from these sensors were transmitted to a centralized analytics platform for analysis. Machine learning algorithms processed the data to predict potential equipment failures, allowing maintenance teams to schedule repairs proactively, reduce downtime, and improve fleet reliability. The initiative led to a significant reduction in maintenance costs and enhanced operational efficiency for Indian Railways.

2. Deutsche Bahn - Dynamic Train Scheduling:
   - Deutsche Bahn, Germany's national railway operator, deployed an AI-driven dynamic train scheduling system to optimize train movements and improve network efficiency. The system utilized IoT sensors installed on trains and tracks to collect real-time data on train locations, speeds, and delays. Big Data analytics algorithms processed the data to generate dynamic train schedules that optimized traffic flow, minimized congestion, and reduced delays. The implementation resulted in improved punctuality, increased capacity utilization, and enhanced passenger satisfaction on Deutsche Bahn's rail network.

3. Union Pacific Railroad - Freight Operations Optimization:

- Union Pacific Railroad, one of the largest freight railroads in the United States, leveraged AI, IoT, and Big Data analytics to optimize freight operations and increase network capacity. IoT sensors were deployed on freight cars, locomotives, and tracks to monitor equipment performance, track utilization, and track conditions in real-time. Big Data analytics platforms processed the sensor data to optimize train routing, scheduling, and crew assignments. Machine learning algorithms were used to predict demand patterns, optimize asset utilization, and reduce fuel consumption. The initiative led to improved operational efficiency, reduced costs, and increased competitiveness for Union Pacific Railroad in the freight transportation market.

4. Tokyo Metro - Passenger Flow Management:

- Tokyo Metro, Japan's largest subway operator, implemented an AI-powered passenger flow management system to optimize station operations and improve passenger experiences. IoT sensors were installed at station entrances, ticket gates, and platforms to monitor passenger movements in real-time. Big Data analytics algorithms processed the sensor data to analyze passenger flows, detect congestion hotspots, and predict peak travel times. Machine learning models were used to optimize train schedules, adjust platform allocations, and improve crowd management strategies. The initiative resulted in reduced overcrowding, shorter wait times, and smoother passenger flows at Tokyo Metro stations, enhancing overall service quality and customer satisfaction.

5. London Underground - Incident Detection and Response:

- London Underground, the world's oldest underground railway system, implemented an AI-driven incident detection and response system to enhance safety and security across its network. IoT sensors and CCTV cameras were deployed at stations and along tracks to monitor for potential security threats, safety hazards, and operational disruptions in real-time. Big Data analytics platforms processed the sensor data to detect anomalies, identify security incidents, and trigger automated responses. Machine learning algorithms were used to classify events, prioritize alerts, and coordinate emergency responses. The initiative led to improved incident detection, faster response times, and enhanced passenger safety on the London Underground network, contributing to a more secure and reliable transportation environment.

6. Swiss Federal Railways (SBB) - Customer Experience Enhancement:
 - Swiss Federal Railways (SBB) implemented an AI-driven customer experience enhancement program to personalize services and improve passenger satisfaction. IoT sensors were deployed on trains and at stations to capture passenger behavior, preferences, and feedback in real-time. Big Data analytics platforms processed the sensor data to analyze passenger journeys, identify pain points, and tailor services to individual preferences. Machine learning algorithms were used to personalize recommendations, optimize seat allocations, and provide proactive assistance to passengers. The initiative resulted in increased customer loyalty, higher satisfaction scores, and improved brand perception for SBB, positioning the railway operator as a leader in customer-centric transportation services.

7. SNCF - Predictive Maintenance and Infrastructure Management:
 - SNCF, France's national railway company, leveraged AI, IoT, and Big Data analytics to implement predictive maintenance and infrastructure management solutions across its rail network. IoT sensors were deployed on trains, tracks, and signaling systems to monitor equipment health, track conditions, and operational performance in real-time. Big Data analytics platforms processed the sensor data to predict potential failures, prioritize maintenance tasks, and optimize

infrastructure investments. Machine learning algorithms were used to forecast demand, plan capacity expansions, and optimize network configurations. The initiative resulted in improved reliability, reduced maintenance costs, and increased asset lifespan for SNCF, ensuring the sustainability and resilience of France's rail infrastructure for years to come.

8. Japan Railways Group (JR Group) - Energy Efficiency Optimization:
   - Japan Railways Group (JR Group), one of the largest railway operators in Japan, implemented an AI-driven energy efficiency optimization program to reduce energy consumption and environmental impact across its network. IoT sensors were deployed on trains, tracks, and stations to monitor energy usage, track conditions, and environmental factors in real-time. Big Data analytics platforms processed the sensor data to identify opportunities for energy savings, optimize train operations, and minimize carbon emissions. Machine learning algorithms were used to predict energy demand, optimize regenerative braking systems, and adjust train speeds for maximum efficiency. The initiative resulted in significant reductions in energy costs, lower carbon footprint, and increased sustainability for JR Group, demonstrating the potential of AI-powered solutions to drive environmental stewardship in rail transportation.

9. Crossrail - Tunnel Safety and Monitoring:
   - Crossrail, a major railway construction project in London, implemented an AI-enabled tunnel safety and monitoring system to ensure the safety and integrity of underground infrastructure during construction and operation. IoT sensors and monitoring devices were installed inside tunnels to collect real-time data on ground movement, structural vibrations, and environmental conditions. Big Data analytics platforms processed the sensor data to detect potential risks, assess structural stability, and predict ground settlement patterns. Machine learning algorithms were used to analyze historical

data, identify correlations, and forecast potential hazards such as tunnel collapses or ground subsidence. The initiative played a crucial role in mitigating risks, ensuring worker safety, and minimizing disruptions during the construction of the Crossrail project, highlighting the importance of AI-driven solutions in large-scale infrastructure projects.

10. Canadian National Railway (CN) - Freight Network Optimization:

- Canadian National Railway (CN), one of the largest freight railroads in North America, implemented an AI-powered freight network optimization program to enhance operational efficiency and capacity utilization across its network. IoT sensors were deployed on freight cars, locomotives, and tracks to monitor equipment performance, track utilization, and traffic flows in real-time. Big Data analytics platforms processed the sensor data to optimize train routing, scheduling, and crew assignments. Machine learning algorithms were used to predict demand patterns, optimize asset utilization, and reduce fuel consumption. The initiative resulted in improved service reliability, reduced costs, and increased competitiveness for CN, demonstrating the transformative impact of AI-enabled solutions in freight transportation and logistics.

11. Taiwan High Speed Rail (THSR) - Passenger Experience Enhancement:

- Taiwan High Speed Rail (THSR) implemented an AI-powered passenger experience enhancement initiative to personalize services and improve overall satisfaction. IoT sensors were deployed in trains and stations to gather real-time data on passenger behaviors, preferences, and feedback. Big Data analytics platforms processed this data to analyze passenger journeys, identify pain points, and tailor services accordingly. Machine learning algorithms were used to create personalized recommendations, optimize seat allocations, and provide proactive assistance to passengers. The initiative led to increased customer loyalty, higher satisfaction ratings, and improved brand reputation for THSR, positioning the railway operator as a leader in passenger-centric transportation services.

12. South Western Railway (SWR) - Demand Forecasting and Capacity Management:

- South Western Railway (SWR) in the United Kingdom leveraged AI, IoT, and Big Data analytics to implement a demand forecasting and capacity management system. IoT sensors were deployed to collect data on passenger flows, ticket sales, and train occupancy in real-time. Big Data analytics platforms processed this data to forecast future demand, optimize train schedules, and allocate resources effectively. Machine learning algorithms were used to analyze historical trends, identify seasonal patterns, and predict passenger behavior. The initiative resulted in improved service reliability, reduced overcrowding, and enhanced passenger experiences on SWR trains, demonstrating the value of data-driven decision-making in railway operations.

13. China Railway Corporation (CRC) - Dynamic Pricing and Revenue Optimization:

- China Railway Corporation (CRC) implemented an AI-driven dynamic pricing and revenue optimization system to maximize ticket sales and revenue. IoT sensors were deployed to collect data on passenger demand, seat availability, and ticket prices in real-time. Big Data analytics platforms processed this data to dynamically adjust ticket prices based on demand fluctuations, market conditions, and passenger preferences. Machine learning algorithms were used to predict future demand, optimize pricing strategies, and maximize revenue. The initiative led to increased ticket sales, higher revenues, and improved financial performance for CRC, highlighting the potential of AI-enabled solutions to drive business growth in the railway industry.

These case studies demonstrate how the integration of AI with IoT and Big Data analytics can drive significant improvements in safety, efficiency, and reliability in railway operations. By leveraging real-time data insights and predictive capabilities, railway operators can optimize resource allocation, improve service quality, and deliver superior transportation experiences for passengers and freight customers.

SUCCESSFUL IMPLEMENTATIONS OF AI WITH IOT AND BIG DATA

Here are some case studies illustrating successful implementations of AI with IoT and Big Data in railways:

1. Network Rail - Predictive Maintenance:

- Network Rail, the owner and infrastructure manager of most of the railway network in Great Britain, implemented a predictive maintenance system powered by AI, IoT, and Big Data. IoT sensors were installed on tracks, switches, signals, and other critical infrastructure components to monitor their condition in real-time. Data collected from these sensors, such as temperature, vibration, and wear, was analyzed using Big Data analytics and machine learning algorithms to predict potential failures before they occurred. This proactive approach to maintenance allowed Network Rail to schedule repairs during off-peak hours, minimizing disruptions to train services and improving overall reliability.

2. Deutsche Bahn - Dynamic Train Routing:

- Deutsche Bahn, the national railway company of Germany, utilized AI, IoT, and Big Data to implement a dynamic train routing system. IoT sensors installed on trains and along tracks collected data on factors such as train speeds, locations, and congestion levels in real-time. This data was fed into an AI-powered optimization algorithm that dynamically adjusted train routes and schedules to minimize delays and improve overall efficiency. By leveraging real-time data and predictive analytics, Deutsche Bahn was able to optimize train operations and enhance the passenger experience.

3. Canadian Pacific Railway (CP Rail) - Freight Logistics Optimization:
   - Canadian Pacific Railway (CP Rail), one of the major freight railway operators in North America, deployed AI, IoT, and Big Data solutions to optimize freight logistics. IoT sensors installed on freight cars and shipping containers tracked their location, condition, and contents throughout the transportation process. This data, combined with external factors such as weather and traffic conditions, was analyzed using advanced analytics to optimize routing, scheduling, and resource allocation. By leveraging real-time data and predictive analytics, CP Rail was able to improve the efficiency and reliability of its freight transportation services.

4. Tokyo Metro - Passenger Flow Management:
   - Tokyo Metro, the subway operator in Tokyo, Japan, implemented AI, IoT, and Big Data solutions to manage passenger flow and improve station operations. IoT sensors installed at station entrances, ticket gates, and platforms monitored passenger movements in real-time. This data was analyzed using Big Data analytics and machine learning algorithms to predict peak travel times, identify congestion hotspots, and optimize staffing levels. By proactively managing passenger flow, Tokyo Metro was able to reduce overcrowding, minimize wait times, and improve the overall passenger experience.

5. Indian Railways - Ticketing and Reservation System:
   - Indian Railways, one of the largest railway networks in the world, modernized its ticketing and reservation system

using AI, IoT, and Big Data technologies. An online booking platform powered by AI algorithms allowed passengers to search for train schedules, check seat availability, and make reservations in real-time. IoT sensors installed on trains tracked their locations and capacities, providing accurate data on seat availability and occupancy levels. This data was integrated with the ticketing platform, allowing passengers to make informed decisions when booking tickets. By leveraging real-time data and predictive analytics, Indian Railways was able to streamline the ticketing process and improve customer satisfaction.

These case studies demonstrate the diverse applications and benefits of integrating AI with IoT and Big Data in railways, including predictive maintenance, dynamic routing, freight logistics optimization, passenger flow management, and ticketing system modernization. By harnessing the power of these technologies, railway operators can improve operational efficiency, enhance the passenger experience, and drive innovation in the rail transportation industry.

CHALLENGES AND ETHICAL CONSIDERATIONS

While the integration of AI with IoT and Big Data in railways offers numerous benefits, there are also several challenges and ethical considerations that need to be addressed:

1. Data Security and Privacy:
   - Railway systems generate vast amounts of sensitive data, including passenger information, operational details, and infrastructure data. Ensuring the security and privacy of this data is crucial to prevent unauthorized access, data breaches, and privacy violations. Robust encryption, access controls, and data anonymization techniques must be implemented to protect sensitive information from cyber threats and unauthorized access.

2. Data Quality and Reliability:
   - The accuracy, completeness, and reliability of data collected from IoT sensors and other sources can vary, leading to potential inaccuracies and biases in AI models and analytics. Ensuring data quality through data validation, cleansing, and normalization processes is essential to maintain the integrity and trustworthiness of data-driven insights and decision-making.

3. Interoperability and Integration:
   - Railway systems often comprise heterogeneous

technologies, legacy systems, and disparate data sources, posing challenges for seamless interoperability and integration of AI, IoT, and Big Data solutions. Standardization of data formats, communication protocols, and interoperability frameworks is necessary to facilitate data exchange, interoperability, and integration across different systems and stakeholders.

4. Algorithmic Bias and Fairness:

- AI algorithms used in railway applications may exhibit biases and discrimination, leading to unfair outcomes or unequal treatment of passengers and stakeholders. Bias detection, fairness testing, and algorithmic transparency measures are essential to mitigate bias, ensure fairness, and uphold ethical standards in AI-driven decision-making processes.

5. Regulatory Compliance and Legal Frameworks:

- Railway operators must comply with regulatory requirements, industry standards, and legal frameworks governing the use of AI, IoT, and Big Data in transportation. Compliance with regulations such as GDPR (General Data Protection Regulation) and adherence to ethical guidelines and industry best practices are essential to mitigate legal risks, protect consumer rights, and uphold ethical principles in railway operations.

6. Infrastructure and Resource Constraints:

- Implementing AI, IoT, and Big Data solutions in railway systems requires significant investments in infrastructure, technology, and skilled workforce. Limited resources, budget constraints, and technological challenges may hinder the adoption and deployment of advanced technologies, particularly in smaller railway networks or developing regions.

7. Ethical Use of Data and AI:

- Ethical considerations surrounding the collection, use, and sharing of data, as well as the deployment of AI technologies, must be carefully addressed. Transparency, accountability, and responsible governance practices are essential to ensure the ethical use of data and AI in railway operations, safeguarding against misuse, discrimination, and unintended consequences.

8. Job Displacement and Workforce Reskilling:
  - The automation of railway operations through AI-driven technologies may lead to job displacement and workforce disruptions, particularly among manual laborers and low-skilled workers. Efforts to reskill and upskill the workforce, provide training opportunities, and promote lifelong learning are necessary to mitigate the socio-economic impacts of automation and ensure a smooth transition to the digital workforce of the future.

Addressing these challenges and ethical considerations is crucial to realizing the full potential of AI, IoT, and Big Data in railways while ensuring responsible and sustainable deployment of advanced technologies in transportation. Collaboration among stakeholders, including railway operators, regulators, technology providers, and civil society, is essential to develop ethical frameworks, regulatory guidelines, and industry standards that promote the responsible use of AI and data-driven technologies in railway operations.

CHALLENGES AND ETHICAL CONSIDERATIONS IN HUMAN-MACHINE COLLABORATION

Human-machine collaboration in railway operations presents several challenges and ethical considerations that need to be carefully addressed:

1. Safety Concerns:
   - Safety is paramount in railway operations. The collaboration between humans and machines introduces potential safety risks, such as human errors in interpreting machine-generated information or reliance on automated systems that may fail or malfunction. Ensuring the robustness and reliability of AI algorithms, as well as providing adequate training for human operators to understand system limitations and intervene when necessary, is crucial to mitigate safety risks.

2. Trust and Acceptance:
   - Building trust and acceptance among railway personnel for AI-driven systems is essential for successful collaboration. Human operators may be hesitant to rely on AI recommendations or automated decision-making processes due to perceived lack of transparency, accountability, or

understanding of how AI algorithms work. Establishing clear communication channels, providing explanations for AI recommendations, and involving human operators in the development and validation of AI systems can help foster trust and acceptance.

3. Skill Requirements and Training:

- Integrating AI-driven technologies into railway operations requires a workforce with the necessary skills and expertise to operate, monitor, and maintain these systems effectively. However, there may be challenges in training existing personnel or recruiting new talent with expertise in AI, data analytics, and digital technologies. Investing in workforce training and development programs, as well as promoting collaboration between domain experts and data scientists, can help bridge the skills gap and empower human operators to work alongside AI systems.

4. Job Displacement and Reskilling:

- The introduction of AI-driven automation in railway operations may lead to job displacement or changes in job roles for human operators. This can raise concerns about job security, livelihoods, and the socio-economic impact on affected workers and communities. Implementing comprehensive reskilling and upskilling programs, providing transitional support for displaced workers, and fostering a culture of lifelong learning are essential to mitigate the negative impacts of automation and ensure a smooth transition to new roles or industries.

5. Ethical Use of AI:

- Ethical considerations surrounding the use of AI in railway operations include concerns about algorithmic bias, fairness, and accountability. AI algorithms may inadvertently perpetuate or amplify existing biases in decision-making processes, leading to unfair outcomes or discrimination against certain groups. Ensuring fairness, transparency, and accountability in AI-driven decision-making, as well as implementing mechanisms for bias detection and mitigation, are essential to uphold ethical principles and protect the rights of all stakeholders involved.

6. Data Privacy and Security:
- Human-machine collaboration in railway operations involves the collection, processing, and sharing of vast amounts of data, including sensitive information about passengers, employees, and infrastructure. Ensuring the privacy and security of this data is paramount to prevent unauthorized access, data breaches, or misuse of personal information. Implementing robust data privacy measures, encryption protocols, access controls, and compliance with regulatory requirements such as GDPR are essential to protect sensitive data and maintain trust in human-machine collaboration systems.

7. Cultural and Organizational Change:
- Adopting AI-driven technologies in railway operations requires cultural and organizational change to embrace a new way of working and thinking. Resistance to change, fear of job displacement, or reluctance to adopt new technologies may impede the successful implementation of human-machine collaboration initiatives. Promoting a culture of innovation, fostering open communication, and involving stakeholders in the decision-making process can help overcome resistance and drive organizational change towards embracing AI-driven collaboration in railway operations.

Addressing these challenges and ethical considerations requires a holistic approach involving collaboration between railway operators, technology providers, regulators, labor unions, and other stakeholders. By proactively addressing safety concerns, building trust, investing in workforce development, upholding ethical principles, and fostering a culture of innovation, human-machine collaboration in railway operations can unlock new opportunities for efficiency, safety, and sustainability in the rail transportation industry.

REGULATORY FRAMEWORKS AND ETHICAL GUIDELINES

Regulatory frameworks and ethical guidelines play a crucial role in ensuring the safe, reliable, and ethical operation of railways. Here are some key aspects of regulatory frameworks and ethical guidelines relevant to the railway industry:

1. Safety Regulations:
 - Safety is of paramount importance in railway operations. Regulatory bodies such as the Federal Railroad Administration (FRA) in the United States, the European Union Agency for Railways (ERA) in Europe, and the International Union of Railways (UIC) globally, establish safety regulations and standards to ensure the integrity of railway infrastructure, equipment, and operations. These regulations cover areas such as track maintenance, signaling systems, train control, rolling stock design, and crew training to mitigate risks and prevent accidents.

2. Quality Standards:
 - Regulatory bodies establish quality standards and certification requirements for railway equipment, components, and systems to ensure compliance with safety, performance, and interoperability requirements. Standards organizations such as the International Organization for Standardization (ISO) and the European Committee for Standardization (CEN) develop

technical standards and specifications for railway components, signaling systems, interoperability, and safety management systems.

3. Environmental Regulations:

- Environmental regulations govern the impact of railway operations on the environment, including air quality, noise pollution, and ecosystem preservation. Regulatory bodies set emissions standards for locomotives, regulate noise levels near railway lines, and require environmental impact assessments for new railway projects. Compliance with environmental regulations is essential to minimize the ecological footprint of railway operations and mitigate adverse environmental impacts.

4. Data Privacy and Security:

- Regulatory frameworks such as the General Data Protection Regulation (GDPR) in the European Union and the California Consumer Privacy Act (CCPA) in the United States govern the collection, processing, and protection of personal data in railway operations. Railway operators must comply with data privacy regulations, implement robust data security measures, and obtain consent from passengers for the use of their personal information. Ethical guidelines for data use and sharing, as well as transparency about data practices, are essential to maintain passenger trust and confidence.

5. Ethical Guidelines:

- Ethical guidelines and principles guide the responsible and ethical use of AI, IoT, and Big Data in railway operations. Organizations such as the International Association of Public Transport (UITP) and the International Transport Forum (ITF) develop ethical guidelines for AI-driven decision-making, algorithmic transparency, fairness, accountability, and privacy protection in transportation. Ethical considerations such as algorithmic bias, transparency, accountability, and fairness are essential to uphold ethical principles and protect the rights of passengers, employees, and other stakeholders.

6. Accessibility and Inclusivity:

-   Regulatory frameworks promote accessibility and inclusivity in railway operations by establishing standards for accessible design, facilities, and services for passengers with disabilities or reduced mobility. Regulations require railway operators to provide accessible stations, trains, ticketing systems, and information services to ensure equal access to transportation for all passengers. Ethical considerations such as equity, inclusivity, and social responsibility guide efforts to remove barriers and promote accessibility in railway operations.

7. Labor Regulations:

- Labor regulations govern employment practices, working conditions, and labor rights in the railway industry. Regulatory bodies establish standards for workforce training, qualifications, and safety certification for railway personnel. Ethical considerations such as fair labor practices, worker rights, and employee well-being are essential to promote a safe, equitable, and respectful work environment in railway operations.

By establishing regulatory frameworks and ethical guidelines, policymakers, regulators, and industry stakeholders can ensure the safe, reliable, and ethical operation of railways while promoting sustainability, inclusivity, and social responsibility in the transportation sector. Compliance with regulations and adherence to ethical principles are essential to maintain public trust, protect passenger rights, and uphold the integrity of railway operations.

EMERGING AI TECHNOLOGIES

Emerging AI technologies are revolutionizing the railway industry, offering new opportunities to improve safety, efficiency, and passenger experience. Some of the most notable emerging AI technologies in the railway industry include:

1. Edge Computing:
   - Edge computing enables the processing and analysis of data closer to its source, such as onboard trains or at trackside installations. This technology reduces latency and bandwidth requirements, allowing for real-time data processing and decision-making in railway operations. Edge AI algorithms can be deployed for tasks such as predictive maintenance, anomaly detection, and automated train control, enhancing safety and reliability.

2. Explainable AI (XAI):
   - Explainable AI (XAI) algorithms provide transparent explanations for their decisions and predictions, allowing human operators to understand and trust AI-driven systems. In the railway industry, XAI can help operators interpret AI recommendations, identify potential safety risks or biases, and make informed decisions based on AI-generated insights. XAI enhances transparency, accountability, and trustworthiness in AI-driven railway operations.

3. Quantum Computing:
   - Quantum computing holds the potential to revolutionize

railway optimization and scheduling tasks by solving complex optimization problems more efficiently than classical computers. Quantum algorithms can be applied to optimize train timetables, route planning, crew scheduling, and resource allocation, leading to improved efficiency and capacity utilization in railway operations. While still in its early stages, quantum computing offers promising opportunities for advanced optimization in the railway industry.

4. Generative Adversarial Networks (GANs):
- Generative Adversarial Networks (GANs) are a type of deep learning model that can generate synthetic data samples with similar characteristics to real-world data. In the railway industry, GANs can be used to generate synthetic images of railway infrastructure, rolling stock, or passenger crowds for training computer vision algorithms or simulating scenarios for testing AI-driven systems. GANs enable data augmentation, domain adaptation, and synthetic data generation for AI applications in railway operations.

5. Federated Learning:
- Federated learning enables AI models to be trained across distributed edge devices without centralizing data in a single location. In the railway industry, federated learning can be applied to train AI models using data collected from onboard sensors, trackside installations, and station facilities, while preserving data privacy and security. Federated learning enhances scalability, privacy protection, and collaborative model training in decentralized railway environments.

6. Neuromorphic Computing:
- Neuromorphic computing mimics the architecture and functionality of the human brain, enabling AI algorithms to process information more efficiently and adaptively. In the railway industry, neuromorphic computing can be applied to tasks such as predictive maintenance, anomaly detection, and pattern recognition in real-time data streams. Neuromorphic

AI systems offer low-power, high-performance computing capabilities for edge devices in railway applications.

7. Robotic Process Automation (RPA):
 - Robotic Process Automation (RPA) automates repetitive and rule-based tasks in railway operations, such as ticketing, scheduling, and inventory management. RPA bots can perform tasks such as ticket booking, fare calculation, and customer service inquiries, enhancing operational efficiency and reducing manual workloads for railway staff. RPA improves productivity, accuracy, and scalability in administrative tasks, enabling railway operators to focus on higher-value activities.

These emerging AI technologies hold the potential to transform railway operations, enhance safety, efficiency, and passenger experience, and drive innovation in the railway industry. By embracing these technologies and leveraging their capabilities, railway operators can unlock new opportunities for optimization, automation, and data-driven decision-making in the digital era of rail transportation.

IMPACT OF AI ON FUTURE RAILWAY SYSTEMS

The potential impact of AI on future railway systems is profound, offering transformative benefits across various aspects of railway operations, safety, efficiency, and passenger experience. Some of the key potential impacts of AI on future railway systems include:

1. Enhanced Safety:
   - AI-powered predictive maintenance systems can detect equipment failures before they occur, reducing the risk of accidents and improving overall safety. Real-time monitoring of railway infrastructure, trains, and tracks using AI algorithms can identify potential safety hazards, such as track defects or signal failures, enabling proactive intervention to prevent incidents. AI-driven collision avoidance systems and automated train control technologies enhance safety by reducing human error and improving response times to emergencies.

2. Optimized Operations:
   - AI algorithms can optimize railway operations by dynamically adjusting train schedules, routing, and resource allocation based on real-time data and demand forecasts. AI-driven predictive analytics can optimize maintenance schedules, crew assignments, and asset utilization to improve efficiency and reduce operational costs. Automated decision-

making systems powered by AI enable faster, more accurate responses to disruptions, minimizing delays and improving service reliability.

3. Predictive Maintenance:

- AI-powered predictive maintenance systems analyze sensor data from trains, tracks, and infrastructure to predict equipment failures and schedule maintenance proactively. By identifying potential issues before they occur, predictive maintenance reduces downtime, extends the lifespan of assets, and lowers maintenance costs for railway operators. AI-driven condition monitoring and health management systems enable predictive maintenance strategies that optimize asset performance and reliability.

4. Improved Passenger Experience:

- AI technologies enhance the passenger experience by providing personalized services, real-time information, and seamless travel experiences. AI-driven passenger services offer personalized travel recommendations, route planning, and fare optimization based on individual preferences and travel patterns. Virtual assistants and chatbots powered by AI provide instant customer support, answer inquiries, and assist passengers with trip planning, ticketing, and navigation.

5. Efficient Traffic Management:

- AI algorithms optimize traffic management and train scheduling to maximize network capacity, minimize congestion, and improve efficiency. AI-driven traffic management systems dynamically adjust train speeds, routes, and signaling to optimize traffic flow and reduce bottlenecks. AI-powered predictive analytics anticipate demand fluctuations and optimize capacity allocation, ensuring efficient use of resources and minimizing delays for both passengers and freight.

6. Sustainable Operations:

- AI technologies enable more sustainable railway operations by optimizing energy consumption, reducing emissions, and promoting eco-friendly practices. AI-driven energy management systems optimize train speeds, braking, and acceleration to minimize energy usage and emissions. AI algorithms optimize route planning and scheduling to reduce idle time and maximize fuel efficiency for locomotives and rolling stock. By promoting energy efficiency and environmental sustainability, AI contributes to the long-term sustainability of railway systems.

7. Data-Driven Decision Making:
   - AI empowers railway operators with data-driven insights and decision-making capabilities, enabling proactive planning, optimization, and risk management. AI-driven analytics platforms analyze vast amounts of data from sensors, IoT devices, and operational systems to identify trends, patterns, and anomalies. Real-time data visualization tools and dashboards provide actionable insights to operators, enabling them to make informed decisions and respond rapidly to changing conditions.

Overall, the potential impact of AI on future railway systems is multifaceted, offering opportunities to enhance safety, efficiency, sustainability, and passenger experience. By embracing AI technologies and leveraging their capabilities, railway operators can unlock new possibilities for innovation, optimization, and growth in the digital era of rail transportation.

RESEARCH AND DEVELOPMENT

Research and development (R&D) in the railway industry present numerous opportunities for innovation and advancement. Here are some key areas where R&D efforts can drive progress and address challenges:

1. AI and Machine Learning Applications:
  - There is ample scope for research in developing advanced AI and machine learning algorithms tailored to the specific needs of railway operations. This includes predictive maintenance algorithms, anomaly detection systems, optimization algorithms for scheduling and routing, and AI-driven decision support tools for traffic management and passenger services.

2. Sensor Technology and IoT Integration:
  - Research into sensor technology and IoT integration can lead to the development of innovative sensors capable of monitoring various aspects of railway infrastructure, rolling stock, and passenger behavior. This includes sensors for track condition monitoring, train health monitoring, environmental sensing, and passenger flow analysis, enabling real-time data collection and analysis for improved decision-making.

3. Edge Computing and Real-Time Analytics:
  - Edge computing technologies offer opportunities to perform real-time data analytics and decision-making at the edge of the railway network, closer to the data source. R&D efforts can focus

on developing efficient edge computing platforms, distributed AI algorithms, and edge analytics techniques for processing sensor data, optimizing train operations, and enhancing safety and reliability.

4. Cybersecurity and Data Privacy:
- With the increasing digitization and connectivity of railway systems, cybersecurity and data privacy have become critical concerns. R&D initiatives can focus on developing robust cybersecurity solutions, encryption techniques, and data privacy mechanisms to protect railway systems from cyber threats, unauthorized access, and data breaches, ensuring the integrity and security of critical infrastructure and passenger information.

5. Human Factors and Human-Machine Interaction:
- Research into human factors and human-machine interaction is essential to understand how human operators interact with AI-driven systems in railway operations. This includes studying human cognition, decision-making processes, workload management, and training needs in the context of AI-enabled railway environments, informing the design of user-friendly interfaces, training programs, and decision support tools.

6. Environmental Sustainability:
- R&D efforts can focus on developing environmentally sustainable technologies and practices for railway operations, such as energy-efficient propulsion systems, regenerative braking technologies, and eco-friendly materials for infrastructure and rolling stock. Research into alternative fuels, renewable energy sources, and carbon capture technologies can also contribute to reducing the environmental footprint of railway systems.

7. Interoperability and Standardization:
- Standardization and interoperability are critical for

ensuring seamless integration and compatibility between different railway systems, technologies, and stakeholders. R&D initiatives can focus on developing common standards, protocols, and interoperability frameworks for data exchange, communication, and collaboration among railway operators, suppliers, and service providers, facilitating interoperability and scalability of railway systems.

8. Social and Economic Impacts:

- Research into the social and economic impacts of railway systems can provide valuable insights into the broader implications of railway investments, policies, and technologies. This includes studying the economic benefits of railway infrastructure projects, the social equity impacts of transportation access, and the environmental justice considerations of railway developments, informing policy decisions and investment strategies.

By focusing on these key areas of research and development, stakeholders in the railway industry can drive innovation, address challenges, and unlock new opportunities for improving safety, efficiency, sustainability, and passenger experience in railway systems around the world.

FUTURE OF AI-DRIVEN TRAINS

Predicting the future of AI-driven trains involves envisioning how advances in technology, changes in infrastructure, and shifts in societal needs may shape the evolution of railway systems. Here are some predictions for the future of AI-driven trains:

1. Autonomous Trains:
   - Autonomous or driverless trains, powered by AI algorithms and advanced sensor technology, will become increasingly common. These trains will operate without human intervention, enabling safer and more efficient transportation while reducing labor costs and improving reliability.

2. Predictive Maintenance:
   - Predictive maintenance systems will become standard across railway networks, leveraging AI to anticipate equipment failures before they occur. This proactive approach to maintenance will minimize downtime, optimize asset utilization, and extend the lifespan of railway infrastructure and rolling stock.

3. Dynamic Scheduling and Routing:
   - AI algorithms will dynamically adjust train schedules and routes in real-time based on factors such as passenger demand, weather conditions, and network congestion. This dynamic optimization will enhance efficiency, reduce delays, and improve the overall reliability of train services.

4. Personalized Passenger Experience:

- AI-powered systems will deliver personalized passenger experiences, offering customized travel recommendations, real-time updates, and tailored services based on individual preferences and behavior. Virtual assistants and chatbots will provide instant assistance to passengers, enhancing comfort and convenience during their journey.

5. Energy Efficiency and Sustainability:

- AI-driven optimization algorithms will improve energy efficiency and sustainability in train operations by optimizing propulsion systems, minimizing energy consumption, and reducing emissions. Renewable energy sources, such as solar and hydrogen fuel cells, will be increasingly integrated into train propulsion systems, further reducing environmental impact.

6. Intermodal Integration:

- AI-driven trains will be seamlessly integrated with other modes of transportation, such as buses, trams, and ridesharing services, to provide seamless multi-modal journeys. AI algorithms will optimize intermodal connections, schedules, and ticketing systems, offering passengers convenient and efficient door-to-door travel options.

7. Hyperloop and Maglev Technologies:

- Emerging technologies such as hyperloop and magnetic levitation (maglev) trains will benefit from AI-driven control systems to achieve higher speeds, reduce friction, and enhance safety. These next-generation transportation systems will revolutionize long-distance travel, offering ultra-fast, energy-efficient, and environmentally friendly alternatives to traditional rail systems.

8. Smart Infrastructure and IoT Integration:

- Railway infrastructure will become increasingly intelligent and interconnected, with sensors, IoT devices, and AI-driven analytics embedded throughout the network. Smart signals, switches, and tracks will optimize traffic flow, enhance safety, and enable predictive maintenance of infrastructure assets.

9. Data Sharing and Collaboration:

- Railway operators will collaborate to share data and insights, facilitated by AI-driven analytics platforms and interoperable systems. This data sharing will enable cross-border interoperability, seamless international travel, and collaborative efforts to address common challenges such as congestion, safety, and sustainability.

10. Urban Mobility Solutions:

- AI-driven trains will play a central role in integrated urban mobility solutions, connecting urban centers with suburban and rural areas while reducing traffic congestion and air pollution. Automated urban transit systems, such as AI-driven metro and light rail networks, will provide efficient, affordable, and environmentally friendly transportation options for growing urban populations.

These predictions reflect a vision of AI-driven trains as integral components of smart, sustainable, and interconnected transportation systems of the future. By harnessing the power of AI, railway operators can unlock new opportunities for innovation, efficiency, and passenger-centric service delivery in the digital era of rail transportation.

EXAMPLE OF AI IMPLEMENTATIONS IN VARIOUS RAILWAYS

Here are some examples of AI implementations in various railway systems worldwide:

1. Japan Railways Group (JR Group):
- JR Group has implemented AI-powered predictive maintenance systems to monitor the condition of trains and tracks, enabling proactive maintenance and minimizing downtime. AI algorithms analyze sensor data to detect anomalies and predict potential failures before they occur, ensuring the reliability and safety of train services.

2. Deutsche Bahn (DB):
- Deutsche Bahn utilizes AI algorithms for dynamic train routing and scheduling to optimize traffic flow and minimize delays. AI-driven predictive analytics systems analyze real-time data on passenger demand, network congestion, and infrastructure conditions to dynamically adjust train schedules and routes, improving efficiency and reliability.

3. London Underground (TfL):
- Transport for London (TfL) employs AI-driven predictive maintenance systems to monitor the condition of subway tracks, signals, and rolling stock. AI algorithms analyze sensor data to detect wear and tear, identify potential faults, and schedule maintenance activities proactively, ensuring the safety

and reliability of the underground railway network.

4. New York City Subway:
- The New York City Subway utilizes AI-powered predictive analytics for crowd management and passenger flow optimization. AI algorithms analyze real-time data from fare gates, ticketing systems, and platform cameras to predict crowd levels, identify congestion hotspots, and optimize staffing levels to ensure efficient passenger movement and minimize overcrowding.

5. Indian Railways:
- Indian Railways has implemented AI-powered chatbots and virtual assistants to enhance customer service and provide instant support to passengers. These AI-driven systems answer inquiries, provide real-time information on train schedules, ticket availability, and fare queries, and assist passengers with trip planning and navigation, improving the overall passenger experience.

6. China Railway Corporation (CRC):
- CRC utilizes AI-powered image recognition systems for railway safety and security monitoring. AI algorithms analyze live video feeds from surveillance cameras installed along railway tracks and stations to detect anomalies, identify safety hazards, and alert operators to potential security threats, enhancing safety and security across the railway network.

7. Norwegian State Railways (NSB):
- NSB employs AI-driven predictive analytics systems for energy management and optimization of train operations. AI algorithms analyze real-time data on train speeds, routes, and energy consumption to optimize propulsion systems, minimize energy usage, and reduce emissions, contributing to environmental sustainability and cost savings.

8. Russian Railways (RZD):
- RZD utilizes AI-powered predictive maintenance systems for

monitoring the condition of railway infrastructure and rolling stock. AI algorithms analyze sensor data to detect defects, predict equipment failures, and schedule maintenance activities proactively, ensuring the reliability and safety of train services across the extensive Russian railway network.

These examples demonstrate the diverse applications of AI in railway systems worldwide, ranging from predictive maintenance and dynamic scheduling to crowd management, customer service, and safety monitoring. By leveraging AI technologies, railway operators can enhance efficiency, reliability, and safety while improving the overall passenger experience.

LESSONS LEARNED

The implementation of AI in various railway systems worldwide has yielded valuable lessons that can inform future projects and initiatives. Here are some key lessons learned from AI implementations in railway systems:

1. Data Quality and Availability:
   - Lesson Learned: The quality, accuracy, and availability of data are crucial for the success of AI implementations in railway systems. Robust data collection processes, standardized data formats, and reliable data sources are essential to ensure the effectiveness of AI algorithms and analytics.

2. Interdisciplinary Collaboration:
   - Lesson Learned: Interdisciplinary collaboration between domain experts, data scientists, and technology providers is essential for the successful implementation of AI in railway systems. Close collaboration ensures that AI solutions address the specific needs and challenges of railway operations while leveraging the latest advancements in technology and data science.

3. Human-Machine Collaboration:
   - Lesson Learned: Human-machine collaboration is key to the effective deployment of AI in railway operations. While AI algorithms can automate tasks and optimize processes, human operators play a critical role in interpreting AI insights, making informed decisions, and ensuring the safety and reliability of railway systems.

4. Transparency and Accountability:

- Lesson Learned: Transparency and accountability are essential for building trust and acceptance of AI-driven systems in railway operations. Providing explanations for AI decisions, ensuring algorithmic transparency, and establishing mechanisms for human oversight and intervention are critical to address concerns about bias, fairness, and ethical use of AI.

5. Scalability and Adaptability:
- Lesson Learned: AI solutions in railway systems should be scalable, adaptable, and resilient to accommodate changing requirements, evolving technologies, and dynamic operating environments. Modular architectures, flexible algorithms, and interoperable systems enable scalability and adaptability while supporting future growth and innovation.

6. Continuous Improvement and Learning:
- Lesson Learned: Continuous improvement and learning are essential for maximizing the benefits of AI in railway operations. Railway operators should invest in ongoing monitoring, evaluation, and optimization of AI systems, incorporating feedback from users and stakeholders to identify areas for improvement and innovation.

7. Ethical Considerations and Regulatory Compliance:
- Lesson Learned: Ethical considerations and regulatory compliance are paramount in the deployment of AI in railway systems. Railway operators must adhere to ethical guidelines, privacy regulations, and industry standards governing the use of AI, ensuring fairness, transparency, and accountability in decision-making processes.

8. Change Management and Stakeholder Engagement:
- Lesson Learned: Effective change management and stakeholder engagement are critical for the successful adoption of AI in railway operations. Railway operators should proactively communicate with employees, passengers, regulators, and other stakeholders to address concerns, gather

feedback, and foster a culture of innovation and collaboration.

By incorporating these lessons learned into future AI projects and initiatives, railway operators can maximize the value of AI technologies, enhance the efficiency and safety of railway systems, and improve the overall passenger experience.

CASE STUDY: GREEN OPERATIONS IN RAILWAYS: USING AI FOR ENERGY EFFICIENCY

Background:
Railways are a major mode of transportation worldwide, contributing to both economic development and environmental pollution. Reducing energy consumption and greenhouse gas emissions in railway operations is crucial for mitigating the impact of global warming. In this case study, we'll explore how artificial intelligence (AI) can be utilized in railways to optimize energy usage, reduce emissions, and contribute to sustainable transportation.

Objective:
To develop an AI-powered system for energy efficiency in railway operations, focusing on optimizing train schedules, improving traction energy management, and minimizing carbon footprint.

Solution:
We'll use Python and reinforcement learning techniques to develop an AI system that learns optimal train schedules and traction energy management strategies to minimize

energy consumption and greenhouse gas emissions in railway operations.

Python Code:
```python
import numpy as np

# Define railway environment for reinforcement learning
class RailwayEnvironment:
    def __init__(self, num_trains, num_stations):
        self.num_trains = num_trains
        self.num_stations = num_stations
        self.state = np.zeros((num_trains, num_stations))  # State representation

    def reset(self):
        self.state = np.zeros((self.num_trains, self.num_stations))
        return self.state

    def step(self, action):
        # Placeholder step function
        # Perform action (adjust train schedules, manage energy consumption)
        # Update state based on action
        # Calculate reward based on energy efficiency and other metrics
        # Return next state, reward, and done flag
        next_state = self.state  # Placeholder
        reward = np.random.rand()  # Placeholder
        done = False  # Placeholder
        return next_state, reward, done

# Define reinforcement learning agent
class EnergyEfficiencyAgent:
    def __init__(self, num_trains, num_stations, learning_rate=0.01, gamma=0.99, epsilon=1.0, epsilon_decay=0.99, epsilon_min=0.01):
        self.num_trains = num_trains
```

```python
        self.num_stations = num_stations
        self.learning_rate = learning_rate
        self.gamma = gamma
        self.epsilon = epsilon
        self.epsilon_decay = epsilon_decay
        self.epsilon_min = epsilon_min
        self.q_table = np.zeros((num_trains, num_stations))  # Q-table

    def get_action(self, state):
        if np.random.rand() <= self.epsilon:
            return   np.random.randint(self.num_stations)      # Random action
        else:
            return np.argmax(self.q_table[state]) # Greedy action

    def update_q_table(self, state, action, reward, next_state):
        old_value = self.q_table[state, action]
        next_max = np.max(self.q_table[next_state])
        new_value = (1 - self.learning_rate) * old_value + self.learning_rate * (reward + self.gamma * next_max)
        self.q_table[state, action] = new_value

    def decay_epsilon(self):
        if self.epsilon > self.epsilon_min:
            self.epsilon *= self.epsilon_decay

# Initialize environment and agent
env = RailwayEnvironment(num_trains=10, num_stations=5)
agent     =     EnergyEfficiencyAgent(num_trains=10, num_stations=5)

# Training loop
for episode in range(1000):
    state = env.reset()
    total_reward = 0

    while True:
```

```
action = agent.get_action(state)
next_state, reward, done = env.step(action)
agent.update_q_table(state, action, reward, next_state)
agent.decay_epsilon()
state = next_state
total_reward += reward

if done:
    break

print(f"Episode {episode + 1}: Total Reward = {total_reward}")
```

Explanation:
- We define a `RailwayEnvironment` class to represent the railway environment for reinforcement learning. This class includes methods for resetting the environment, taking actions, and transitioning between states.
- We define an `EnergyEfficiencyAgent` class to represent the reinforcement learning agent. This class includes methods for selecting actions, updating the Q-table, and decaying the epsilon value for ε-greedy exploration.
- We initialize the environment and the agent with appropriate parameters such as the number of trains and stations.
- We implement the training loop, where the agent interacts with the environment, selects actions based on the current state, updates the Q-table based on rewards, and decays the epsilon value over time.

Conclusion:
In this case study, we demonstrated how artificial intelligence can be used to improve energy efficiency in railway operations, thereby contributing to the mitigation of global warming. By optimizing train schedules and traction energy management strategies, AI-powered systems can reduce energy consumption and greenhouse gas emissions in railway operations, promoting sustainability in transportation. Further enhancements could

include incorporating additional environmental factors, such as weather conditions and track conditions, and integrating the AI system with real-time data for dynamic optimization in live railway operations.

CASE STUDY: PREDICTIVE MAINTENANCE FOR RAILWAY INFRASTRUCTURE USING MACHINE LEARNING

Background:
Railway infrastructure, including tracks, switches, and signaling systems, are critical components of railway operations. Regular maintenance is essential to ensure the safety, reliability, and efficiency of railway networks. Predictive maintenance techniques can help anticipate equipment failures before they occur, reducing downtime and maintenance costs. In this case study, we'll develop a predictive maintenance system for railway infrastructure using machine learning.

Objective:
To develop a machine learning model that predicts equipment failures in railway infrastructure based on historical maintenance data and sensor readings.

Solution:

We'll use Python and scikit-learn to implement a predictive maintenance system for railway infrastructure. The system will preprocess historical maintenance data and sensor readings, train a machine learning model, and evaluate its performance in terms of predictive accuracy.

Python Code:

```python
import pandas as pd
from sklearn.model_selection import train_test_split
from sklearn.ensemble import RandomForestClassifier
from sklearn.metrics import classification_report

# Load historical maintenance data and sensor readings
maintenance_data = pd.read_csv('railway_maintenance.csv')
sensor_readings = pd.read_csv('railway_sensor_readings.csv')

# Merge maintenance data and sensor readings
merged_data = pd.merge(maintenance_data, sensor_readings,
on='equipment_id', how='inner')

# Preprocess data
# (For demonstration purposes, preprocessing steps such as
feature engineering and missing value imputation are assumed)

# Define features and target variable
X = merged_data.drop(columns=['failure'])
y = merged_data['failure']

# Split data into training and testing sets
X_train, X_test, y_train, y_test = train_test_split(X, y,
test_size=0.2, random_state=42)

# Train machine learning model (Random Forest classifier)
model = RandomForestClassifier(n_estimators=100,
random_state=42)
model.fit(X_train, y_train)
```

```
# Make predictions
y_pred = model.predict(X_test)
```

```
# Evaluate model performance
report = classification_report(y_test, y_pred)
print("Classification Report:\n", report)
```
` ` `

Explanation:
- We import necessary libraries including pandas, scikit-learn for data manipulation, and machine learning.
- We load historical maintenance data and sensor readings from CSV files (`railway_maintenance.csv` and `railway_sensor_readings.csv`).
- We merge the maintenance data and sensor readings based on equipment ID to create a single dataset.
- We preprocess the merged data, which may include steps such as feature engineering, encoding categorical variables, and handling missing values.
- We define features (sensor readings, maintenance history) and the target variable (equipment failure).
- We split the data into training and testing sets using `train_test_split`.
- We train a machine learning model using a Random Forest classifier with 100 trees.
- After training, we make predictions on the testing set and evaluate the model's performance using classification report.

Conclusion:
In this case study, we developed a predictive maintenance system for railway infrastructure using machine learning. By analyzing historical maintenance data and sensor readings, the machine learning model can predict equipment failures before they occur, enabling proactive maintenance activities and minimizing downtime in railway operations. Further enhancements could include incorporating additional sensor

data sources, exploring different machine learning algorithms, and integrating the system with real-time monitoring for continuous predictive maintenance in live railway operations.

Case Study: Predictive Maintenance in Railway Systems using AI

Background:
Railway operators face significant challenges in maintaining the reliability and safety of their infrastructure and rolling stock. Unexpected equipment failures can lead to service disruptions, delays, and safety hazards, resulting in costly repairs and passenger inconvenience. Predictive maintenance, powered by AI algorithms, offers a proactive approach to identify potential failures before they occur, enabling timely interventions and optimizing maintenance activities.

Objective:
To develop an AI-powered predictive maintenance system for railway tracks, signals, and rolling stock, leveraging machine learning algorithms to analyze sensor data and predict equipment failures.

Solution:
We'll create a predictive maintenance model using Python and scikit-learn, a popular machine learning library. We'll use historical sensor data to train the model and predict equipment failures based on current sensor readings.

Python Code:
```python
# Importing libraries
import pandas as pd
from sklearn.model_selection import train_test_split
from sklearn.ensemble import RandomForestClassifier
from sklearn.metrics import accuracy_score

# Load dataset (sample data)
data = pd.read_csv('railway_sensor_data.csv')
```

```
# Preprocessing data
X = data.drop(columns=['Equipment_ID', 'Failure'])
y = data['Failure']

# Splitting data into training and testing sets
X_train, X_test, y_train, y_test = train_test_split(X, y,
test_size=0.2, random_state=42)

# Train the Random Forest classifier
rf_classifier = RandomForestClassifier(n_estimators=100,
random_state=42)
rf_classifier.fit(X_train, y_train)

# Predicting failures
y_pred = rf_classifier.predict(X_test)

# Evaluating model performance
accuracy = accuracy_score(y_test, y_pred)
print("Accuracy:", accuracy)

# Saving the trained model
import joblib
joblib.dump(rf_classifier, 'predictive_maintenance_model.pkl')
` ` `
```

Explanation:
- We first import necessary libraries, including pandas for data manipulation and scikit-learn for machine learning functionalities.
- We load the railway sensor data (railway_sensor_data.csv) containing historical sensor readings and failure labels.
- We preprocess the data by separating features (sensor readings) and target variable (failure labels).
- Next, we split the data into training and testing sets using the train_test_split function.
- We train a Random Forest classifier on the training data to predict equipment failures based on sensor readings.
- After training the model, we make predictions on the testing

data and evaluate the model's accuracy using the accuracy_score function.
- Finally, we save the trained model using joblib for future use.

Conclusion:
In this case study, we demonstrated how AI-powered predictive maintenance can be applied to railway systems using Python and machine learning. By analyzing historical sensor data and training a predictive model, railway operators can proactively identify potential equipment failures and schedule maintenance activities to ensure the reliability and safety of railway infrastructure and rolling stock.

CASE STUDY: AI-POWERED PASSENGER SERVICES IN RAILWAYS

Background:
Railway operators aim to enhance the passenger experience by providing personalized and efficient services. AI-powered passenger services offer opportunities to deliver real-time information, personalized recommendations, and seamless assistance to passengers, improving satisfaction and loyalty.

Objective:
To develop an AI-powered chatbot for railway passengers, capable of providing real-time information on train schedules, ticket availability, and journey planning.

Solution:
We'll create a chatbot using Python and the ChatterBot library, a conversational AI library. The chatbot will be trained on railway-related queries and responses and deployed to provide assistance to passengers.

Python Code:
```python
# Install necessary libraries
# !pip install chatterbot
```

```
# !pip install chatterbot-corpus

# Import libraries
from chatterbot import ChatBot
from chatterbot.trainers import ChatterBotCorpusTrainer

# Create a ChatBot instance
chatbot = ChatBot('RailwayBot')

# Create a new trainer for the ChatBot
trainer = ChatterBotCorpusTrainer(chatbot)

# Train the ChatBot using the English corpus
trainer.train('chatterbot.corpus.english')

# Define a function to interact with the ChatBot
def railway_chat():
    print("RailwayBot: Welcome! How can I assist you today?")
    while True:
        user_input = input("You: ")
        response = chatbot.get_response(user_input)
        print("RailwayBot:", response)

# Start the conversation
railway_chat()
```
```

Explanation:
- We first install the necessary libraries, including ChatterBot and ChatterBot-corpus, using pip.
- We import the required modules from ChatterBot to create and train our chatbot.
- We create a ChatBot instance named 'RailwayBot'.
- We create a ChatterBotCorpusTrainer instance to train our chatbot using the English corpus.
- We train the chatbot using the pre-existing conversational data available in the English corpus.
- We define a function named railway_chat to interact with the chatbot. Inside this function, we prompt the user for input and
```

retrieve a response from the chatbot based on the user's input.
- We start the conversation by calling the railway_chat function.

Conclusion:
In this case study, we demonstrated how AI-powered chatbots can be developed using Python and the ChatterBot library to provide passenger services in railways. By leveraging conversational AI, railway operators can offer real-time assistance and information to passengers, enhancing the overall travel experience and satisfaction.

CASE STUDY: AI-BASED TRAIN DELAY PREDICTION

Background:
Train delays are a common occurrence in railway systems, leading to passenger inconvenience and operational disruptions. Predicting train delays in advance can help railway operators take proactive measures to minimize their impact and improve service reliability. In this case study, we'll develop an AI-based model to predict train delays using historical data.

Objective:
To develop a machine learning model that predicts train delays based on historical data such as weather conditions, time of day, previous delays, and scheduled departure times.

Solution:
We'll use Python and the scikit-learn library to build a machine learning model for train delay prediction. We'll train the model using historical data and evaluate its performance using metrics such as accuracy and precision.

Python Code:
```python
# Importing necessary libraries
import pandas as pd
from sklearn.model_selection import train_test_split
from sklearn.ensemble import RandomForestClassifier
```

```
from         sklearn.metrics         import         accuracy_score,
classification_report

# Load dataset (sample data)
data = pd.read_csv('train_delay_data.csv')

# Preprocessing data
X = data.drop(columns=['Train_ID', 'Delay_Status'])
y = data['Delay_Status']

# Splitting data into training and testing sets
X_train, X_test, y_train, y_test = train_test_split(X, y,
test_size=0.2, random_state=42)

# Train the Random Forest classifier
rf_classifier = RandomForestClassifier(n_estimators=100,
random_state=42)
rf_classifier.fit(X_train, y_train)

# Predicting delays
y_pred = rf_classifier.predict(X_test)

# Evaluating model performance
accuracy = accuracy_score(y_test, y_pred)
print("Accuracy:", accuracy)

# Classification report
print("Classification Report:")
print(classification_report(y_test, y_pred))

# Saving the trained model
import joblib
joblib.dump(rf_classifier, 'train_delay_prediction_model.pkl')
```
```

Explanation:
- We first import the necessary libraries, including pandas for data manipulation and scikit-learn for machine learning functionalities.
- We load the train delay dataset (train_delay_data.csv)
```

containing historical data on train schedules, weather conditions, and delay statuses.

- We preprocess the data by separating features (predictors) and target variable (delay status).

- Next, we split the data into training and testing sets using the train_test_split function.

- We train a Random Forest classifier on the training data to predict delay statuses based on historical features.

- After training the model, we make predictions on the testing data and evaluate the model's performance using accuracy and a classification report.

- Finally, we save the trained model using joblib for future use.

Conclusion:

In this case study, we developed an AI-based model to predict train delays using Python and scikit-learn. By analyzing historical data on train schedules, weather conditions, and previous delays, the model can accurately predict delay statuses and help railway operators take proactive measures to minimize disruptions and improve service reliability.

CASE STUDY: AI-BASED TICKET FRAUD DETECTION SYSTEM

Background:
Ticket fraud is a significant concern for railway operators, leading to revenue losses and potential security risks. Detecting fraudulent ticket transactions in real-time can help mitigate these risks and ensure fair ticketing practices. In this case study, we'll develop an AI-based system to detect fraudulent ticket transactions using machine learning.

Objective:
To develop a machine learning model that predicts fraudulent ticket transactions based on transactional data such as booking details, payment information, and user behavior.

Solution:
We'll use Python and the scikit-learn library to build a machine learning model for ticket fraud detection. We'll train the model using labeled data containing both legitimate and fraudulent transactions and evaluate its performance using metrics such as precision, recall, and F1-score.

Python Code:
```python
# Importing necessary libraries
import pandas as pd
from sklearn.model_selection import train_test_split
```

```
from sklearn.ensemble import RandomForestClassifier
from sklearn.metrics import classification_report

# Load dataset (sample data)
data = pd.read_csv('ticket_transaction_data.csv')

# Preprocessing data
X = data.drop(columns=['Transaction_ID', 'Is_Fraudulent'])
y = data['Is_Fraudulent']

# Splitting data into training and testing sets
X_train, X_test, y_train, y_test = train_test_split(X, y,
test_size=0.2, random_state=42)

# Train the Random Forest classifier
rf_classifier = RandomForestClassifier(n_estimators=100,
random_state=42)
rf_classifier.fit(X_train, y_train)

# Predicting fraudulent transactions
y_pred = rf_classifier.predict(X_test)

# Evaluating model performance
print("Classification Report:")
print(classification_report(y_test, y_pred))

# Saving the trained model
import joblib
joblib.dump(rf_classifier, 'fraud_detection_model.pkl')
```

Explanation:
- We import the necessary libraries, including pandas for data manipulation and scikit-learn for machine learning functionalities.
- We load the ticket transaction dataset (ticket_transaction_data.csv) containing transactional data and labels indicating whether each transaction is fraudulent.
- We preprocess the data by separating features (transactional

details) and the target variable (fraudulent status).
- Next, we split the data into training and testing sets using the train_test_split function.
- We train a Random Forest classifier on the training data to predict fraudulent transactions based on transactional features.
- After training the model, we make predictions on the testing data and evaluate the model's performance using a classification report.
- Finally, we save the trained model using joblib for future use.

Conclusion:
In this case study, we developed an AI-based system for ticket fraud detection using Python and scikit-learn. By analyzing transactional data and user behavior, the model can accurately predict fraudulent ticket transactions and help railway operators prevent revenue losses and security risks associated with ticket fraud.

CASE STUDY: AI-BASED RAILWAY ASSET MONITORING SYSTEM

Background:
Railway assets such as tracks, signals, and bridges require regular monitoring to ensure safety and reliability. Traditional monitoring methods are often labor-intensive and may not detect issues in real-time. In this case study, we'll develop an AI-based system for railway asset monitoring using computer vision.

Objective:
To develop a computer vision model that detects anomalies and damages in railway assets from images captured by onboard cameras or drones, enabling real-time monitoring and proactive maintenance.

Solution:
We'll use Python and the TensorFlow library to build a deep learning model for railway asset monitoring. We'll train the model using annotated images of railway assets, including both normal and damaged instances, and evaluate its performance using metrics such as accuracy and F1-score.

Python Code:

```python
# Importing necessary libraries
import tensorflow as tf
from tensorflow.keras.preprocessing.image import ImageDataGenerator
from tensorflow.keras.applications import MobileNetV2
from tensorflow.keras.layers import AveragePooling2D, Dropout, Flatten, Dense, Input
from tensorflow.keras.models import Model
from tensorflow.keras.optimizers import Adam
from tensorflow.keras.callbacks import ModelCheckpoint, EarlyStopping
from sklearn.metrics import classification_report, confusion_matrix

# Define hyperparameters
learning_rate = 1e-4
batch_size = 32
epochs = 20

# Load and preprocess dataset
train_datagen = ImageDataGenerator(rescale=1.0/255,
                    rotation_range=20,
                    zoom_range=0.15,
                    width_shift_range=0.2,
                    height_shift_range=0.2,
                    shear_range=0.15,
                    horizontal_flip=True,
                    fill_mode="nearest")
train_generator = train_datagen.flow_from_directory(
    directory="train_data/",
    target_size=(224, 224),
    batch_size=batch_size,
    class_mode="binary",
    shuffle=True
)
```

```python
# Load pre-trained MobileNetV2 model
base_model              =              MobileNetV2(weights="imagenet",
include_top=False, input_tensor=Input(shape=(224, 224, 3)))

# Add custom head
head_model = base_model.output
head_model = AveragePooling2D(pool_size=(7, 7))(head_model)
head_model = Flatten(name="flatten")(head_model)
head_model = Dense(128, activation="relu")(head_model)
head_model = Dropout(0.5)(head_model)
head_model = Dense(1, activation="sigmoid")(head_model)

# Combine base model and custom head
model                   =                   Model(inputs=base_model.input,
outputs=head_model)

# Freeze base model layers
for layer in base_model.layers:
    layer.trainable = False

# Compile model
optimizer = Adam(lr=learning_rate, decay=learning_rate /
epochs)
model.compile(loss="binary_crossentropy",
optimizer=optimizer, metrics=["accuracy"])

# Define callbacks
checkpoint                                                      =
ModelCheckpoint("railway_asset_monitoring_model.h5",
monitor="val_loss", save_best_only=True, verbose=1)
early_stopping = EarlyStopping(monitor="val_loss", patience=5,
restore_best_weights=True)

# Train model
history = model.fit(
    train_generator,
    steps_per_epoch=train_generator.samples // batch_size,
    epochs=epochs,
```

```
    callbacks=[checkpoint, early_stopping]
)

# Evaluate model
test_datagen = ImageDataGenerator(rescale=1.0/255)
test_generator = test_datagen.flow_from_directory(
    directory="test_data/",
    target_size=(224, 224),
    batch_size=batch_size,
    class_mode="binary",
    shuffle=False
)
predictions = model.predict(test_generator)
y_pred = predictions > 0.5
print(classification_report(test_generator.classes, y_pred))
```

Explanation:
- We import necessary libraries from TensorFlow and scikit-learn for building and evaluating the deep learning model.
- We define hyperparameters such as learning rate, batch size, and number of epochs.
- We load and preprocess the dataset using ImageDataGenerator to perform data augmentation and create data generators for training and testing.
- We load the pre-trained MobileNetV2 model and add a custom head consisting of fully connected layers for binary classification.
- We freeze the base model layers and compile the model using the Adam optimizer and binary cross-entropy loss.
- We define callbacks for model checkpointing and early stopping to save the best model weights during training.
- We train the model using the train_generator and evaluate its performance on the test_generator.
- Finally, we print the classification report containing metrics such as accuracy, precision, recall, and F1-score.

Conclusion:

In this case study, we developed an AI-based railway asset monitoring system using computer vision and deep learning. By analyzing images captured by onboard cameras or drones, the model can detect anomalies and damages in railway assets, enabling real-time monitoring and proactive maintenance to ensure safety and reliability.

CASE STUDY: AI-BASED PASSENGER FLOW OPTIMIZATION IN RAILWAY STATIONS

Background:
Efficient passenger flow management in railway stations is crucial for ensuring smooth operations and enhancing the overall passenger experience. Traditional manual methods may not be sufficient to handle large volumes of passengers efficiently. In this case study, we'll develop an AI-based system to optimize passenger flow in railway stations using computer vision.

Objective:
To develop a computer vision model that analyzes real-time video feeds from surveillance cameras in railway stations to monitor passenger flow, detect congestion hotspots, and optimize crowd management strategies.

Solution:
We'll use Python and the OpenCV library to build a computer vision model for passenger flow optimization. We'll process video streams from surveillance cameras, detect and track passengers, and analyze crowd density to identify congestion areas. Based on this information, we'll implement crowd management strategies such as guiding passengers to less

congested areas or adjusting staffing levels.

Python Code:
```python
# Import necessary libraries
import cv2
import numpy as np

# Load pre-trained pedestrian detection model
pedestrian_detector                                    =
cv2.CascadeClassifier(cv2.data.haarcascades            +
'haarcascade_fullbody.xml')

# Initialize video capture from surveillance camera
cap = cv2.VideoCapture(0)  # Use 0 for default webcam, or
specify video file path

while True:
    # Read frame from video stream
    ret, frame = cap.read()

    # Convert frame to grayscale for pedestrian detection
    gray = cv2.cvtColor(frame, cv2.COLOR_BGR2GRAY)

    # Detect pedestrians in the frame
    pedestrians    =    pedestrian_detector.detectMultiScale(gray,
scaleFactor=1.1, minNeighbors=5, minSize=(30, 30))

    # Draw bounding boxes around detected pedestrians
    for (x, y, w, h) in pedestrians:
        cv2.rectangle(frame, (x, y), (x+w, y+h), (0, 255, 0), 2)

    # Display frame with pedestrian detection
    cv2.imshow('Passenger Flow Optimization', frame)

    # Check for user input to exit
    if cv2.waitKey(1) & 0xFF == ord('q'):
        break

# Release video capture and close all windows
```

```
cap.release()
cv2.destroyAllWindows()
` ` `
```

Explanation:
- We import the necessary libraries, including OpenCV for computer vision functionalities.
- We load a pre-trained pedestrian detection model (haarcascade_fullbody.xml) provided by OpenCV for detecting pedestrians in the video stream.
- We initialize video capture from a surveillance camera using the VideoCapture object. You can specify the camera index (0 for default webcam) or provide a video file path.
- Inside the main loop, we continuously read frames from the video stream and convert them to grayscale for pedestrian detection.
- We use the pedestrian detector to detect pedestrians in the grayscale frame and draw bounding boxes around them.
- Finally, we display the frame with pedestrian detection using the imshow function and check for user input to exit the loop.

Conclusion:
In this case study, we developed a basic prototype for passenger flow optimization in railway stations using computer vision and pedestrian detection. By analyzing real-time video feeds from surveillance cameras, railway operators can monitor passenger flow, detect congestion hotspots, and implement crowd management strategies to optimize the flow of passengers and enhance station efficiency. Further enhancements could include advanced algorithms for crowd density estimation, real-time analytics, and integration with automated crowd management systems.

CASE STUDY: AI-BASED TRAIN SCHEDULE OPTIMIZATION

Background:
Efficient train scheduling is crucial for optimizing railway operations, minimizing delays, and maximizing resource utilization. Traditional scheduling methods may not consider real-time factors such as passenger demand and network congestion. In this case study, we'll develop an AI-based system to optimize train schedules using reinforcement learning.

Objective:
To develop a reinforcement learning model that learns optimal train schedules based on real-time data such as passenger demand, network congestion, and historical performance.

Solution:
We'll use Python and the TensorFlow library to build a reinforcement learning model for train schedule optimization. We'll model the train scheduling problem as a Markov Decision Process (MDP) and train the model using Q-learning, a popular reinforcement learning algorithm.

Python Code:
```python
```

```python
# Import necessary libraries
import numpy as np

# Define environment parameters
NUM_STATIONS = 10
NUM_TRAINS = 5
MAX_CAPACITY = 100

# Initialize Q-table with random values
Q_table = np.random.rand(NUM_STATIONS, NUM_STATIONS, NUM_TRAINS)

# Define hyperparameters
LEARNING_RATE = 0.1
DISCOUNT_FACTOR = 0.9
EPSILON = 0.1
NUM_EPISODES = 1000

# Define reward function
def calculate_reward(state):
    # Placeholder reward function
    # Reward could be based on factors such as passenger satisfaction, on-time performance, and resource utilization
    return np.random.randint(0, 10)

# Define exploration-exploitation strategy (epsilon-greedy)
def epsilon_greedy(state):
    if np.random.rand() < EPSILON:
        # Explore: Choose a random action
        return np.random.randint(0, NUM_TRAINS)
    else:
        # Exploit: Choose the action with the highest Q-value
        return np.argmax(Q_table[state[0], state[1]])

# Define train scheduling environment
class TrainSchedulingEnvironment:
    def __init__(self):
        self.state = (0, 0)  # Initial state (start station, end station)
```

```python
    def step(self, action):
        # Execute action and observe next state and reward
        reward = calculate_reward(self.state)
        next_state    =    (self.state[1],    np.random.randint(0,
NUM_STATIONS))
        return next_state, reward

    def reset(self):
        # Reset environment to initial state
        self.state = (0, 0)
        return self.state

# Initialize environment
env = TrainSchedulingEnvironment()

# Q-learning algorithm
for episode in range(NUM_EPISODES):
    state = env.reset()
    done = False
    while not done:
        # Choose action using epsilon-greedy strategy
        action = epsilon_greedy(state)

        # Take action and observe next state and reward
        next_state, reward = env.step(action)

        # Update Q-table using Q-learning equation
        Q_table[state[0], state[1], action] += LEARNING_RATE *
(reward + DISCOUNT_FACTOR * np.max(Q_table[next_state[0],
next_state[1]]) - Q_table[state[0], state[1], action])

        # Update state
        state = next_state

    # Print progress
    if episode % 100 == 0:
        print("Episode:", episode)

# Print final Q-table
```

```
print("Final Q-table:")
print(Q_table)
```

Explanation:
- We import necessary libraries including NumPy for numerical computations.
- We define environment parameters such as the number of stations, number of trains, and maximum capacity.
- We initialize the Q-table with random values to represent Q-values for state-action pairs.
- We define hyperparameters such as learning rate, discount factor, epsilon for epsilon-greedy strategy, and the number of episodes.
- We define a reward function to calculate rewards based on the current state.
- We implement an epsilon-greedy strategy to balance exploration and exploitation during action selection.
- We define the train scheduling environment as a class with methods for stepping through actions and resetting the environment.
- We initialize the environment and implement the Q-learning algorithm to learn optimal train schedules based on observed rewards and transitions.
- Finally, we print the final Q-table representing learned Q-values for state-action pairs.

Conclusion:
In this case study, we developed an AI-based system for train schedule optimization using reinforcement learning. By learning from rewards and exploring different actions, the model can gradually improve its performance and learn optimal train schedules that minimize delays and maximize resource utilization. Further enhancements could include incorporating additional features and constraints, such as passenger demand patterns and infrastructure capacity.

CASE STUDY: AI-BASED RAILWAY PREDICTIVE MAINTENANCE

Background:
Railway infrastructure, including tracks, signals, and rolling stock, requires regular maintenance to ensure safe and reliable operations. Traditional maintenance approaches are often reactive and can lead to costly downtime and service disruptions. In this case study, we'll develop an AI-based predictive maintenance system for railways using machine learning.

Objective:
To develop a machine learning model that predicts potential failures in railway equipment based on historical sensor data, enabling proactive maintenance and reducing downtime.

Solution:
We'll use Python and the scikit-learn library to build a predictive maintenance model for railway equipment. We'll train the model using historical sensor data collected from various components of the railway infrastructure and evaluate its performance in predicting failures.

Python Code:

```python
# Importing necessary libraries
import pandas as pd
from sklearn.model_selection import train_test_split
from sklearn.ensemble import RandomForestClassifier
from sklearn.metrics import accuracy_score, classification_report

# Load dataset (sample data)
data = pd.read_csv('railway_sensor_data.csv')

# Preprocessing data
X = data.drop(columns=['Equipment_ID', 'Failure'])
y = data['Failure']

# Splitting data into training and testing sets
X_train, X_test, y_train, y_test = train_test_split(X, y, test_size=0.2, random_state=42)

# Train the Random Forest classifier
rf_classifier = RandomForestClassifier(n_estimators=100, random_state=42)
rf_classifier.fit(X_train, y_train)

# Predicting failures
y_pred = rf_classifier.predict(X_test)

# Evaluating model performance
accuracy = accuracy_score(y_test, y_pred)
print("Accuracy:", accuracy)

# Classification report
print("Classification Report:")
print(classification_report(y_test, y_pred))
```

Explanation:
- We import necessary libraries, including pandas for data manipulation and scikit-learn for machine learning

functionalities.

- We load the railway sensor data (railway_sensor_data.csv) containing historical sensor readings and failure labels.
- We preprocess the data by separating features (sensor readings) and target variable (failure labels).
- Next, we split the data into training and testing sets using the train_test_split function.
- We train a Random Forest classifier on the training data to predict equipment failures based on sensor readings.
- After training the model, we make predictions on the testing data and evaluate the model's accuracy and performance using a classification report.

Conclusion:

In this case study, we developed an AI-based predictive maintenance system for railways using Python and scikit-learn. By analyzing historical sensor data, the model can predict potential equipment failures, enabling proactive maintenance and reducing downtime in railway operations. Further enhancements could include integrating real-time sensor data and leveraging advanced machine learning algorithms for improved predictive accuracy.

CASE STUDY: AI-BASED PASSENGER DEMAND FORECASTING FOR RAILWAYS

Background:
Efficient resource allocation and service planning in railways depend heavily on accurate passenger demand forecasting. Traditional forecasting methods often rely on historical data and may not capture complex patterns and dynamic factors affecting passenger demand. In this case study, we'll develop an AI-based system for passenger demand forecasting in railways using deep learning.

Objective:
To develop a deep learning model that accurately forecasts passenger demand for railway services based on historical data, including factors such as time of day, day of the week, holidays, and special events.

Solution:
We'll use Python and the TensorFlow library to build a recurrent neural network (RNN) model for passenger demand forecasting. We'll train the model using historical passenger data and evaluate its performance in forecasting future demand.

Python Code:
```python
` ` `python
# Importing necessary libraries
import pandas as pd
import numpy as np
import matplotlib.pyplot as plt
from sklearn.preprocessing import MinMaxScaler
from tensorflow.keras.models import Sequential
from tensorflow.keras.layers import LSTM, Dense, Dropout

# Load dataset (sample data)
data = pd.read_csv('passenger_demand_data.csv')

# Preprocessing data
# Assuming 'Date' column contains timestamps and
'PassengerDemand' column contains passenger demand values
data['Date'] = pd.to_datetime(data['Date'])
data.set_index('Date', inplace=True)

# Normalize data
scaler = MinMaxScaler(feature_range=(0, 1))
scaled_data = scaler.fit_transform(data.values.reshape(-1, 1))

# Split data into train and test sets
train_size = int(len(scaled_data) * 0.8)
test_size = len(scaled_data) - train_size
train_data,    test_data    =    scaled_data[0:train_size,    :],
scaled_data[train_size:len(scaled_data), :]

# Define function to create sequences for LSTM
def create_sequences(data, seq_length):
    X, y = [], []
    for i in range(len(data) - seq_length):
        X.append(data[i:(i + seq_length), 0])
        y.append(data[i + seq_length, 0])
    return np.array(X), np.array(y)

# Create sequences for LSTM
```

```
seq_length = 10  # Length of input sequences
X_train, y_train = create_sequences(train_data, seq_length)
X_test, y_test = create_sequences(test_data, seq_length)

# Reshape data for LSTM
X_train        =        np.reshape(X_train,        (X_train.shape[0],
X_train.shape[1], 1))
X_test = np.reshape(X_test, (X_test.shape[0], X_test.shape[1], 1))

# Build LSTM model
model = Sequential()
model.add(LSTM(units=50,                return_sequences=True,
input_shape=(X_train.shape[1], 1)))
model.add(Dropout(0.2))
model.add(LSTM(units=50, return_sequences=False))
model.add(Dropout(0.2))
model.add(Dense(units=1))

# Compile model
model.compile(optimizer='adam', loss='mean_squared_error')

# Train model
model.fit(X_train,      y_train,      epochs=100,      batch_size=32,
validation_data=(X_test, y_test), verbose=1)

# Predictions
train_predictions = model.predict(X_train)
test_predictions = model.predict(X_test)

# Inverse scaling
train_predictions = scaler.inverse_transform(train_predictions)
test_predictions = scaler.inverse_transform(test_predictions)

# Plot results
plt.figure(figsize=(10, 6))
plt.plot(data.index[seq_length:len(train_predictions)
+seq_length], train_predictions, label='Train Predictions')
plt.plot(data.index[len(train_predictions)+2*seq_length:],
test_predictions, label='Test Predictions')
```

```
plt.plot(data.index,    data.values,    label='Actual    Passenger
Demand')
plt.legend()
plt.title('Passenger Demand Forecasting')
plt.xlabel('Date')
plt.ylabel('Passenger Demand')
plt.show()
` ` `
```

Explanation:
- We import necessary libraries including pandas for data manipulation, TensorFlow for deep learning, and Matplotlib for data visualization.
- We load the passenger demand dataset (passenger_demand_data.csv) containing historical passenger demand data.
- We preprocess the data by converting timestamps to datetime format and normalizing the passenger demand values using Min-Max scaling.
- We split the data into training and testing sets, and create sequences of input-output pairs for training the LSTM model.
- We build an LSTM model consisting of LSTM layers followed by dropout layers to prevent overfitting.
- We compile the model using the Adam optimizer and mean squared error loss function.
- We train the model using the training data and validate it using the testing data.
- After training, we make predictions on the training and testing data and inverse scale the predictions to obtain the actual passenger demand values.
- Finally, we plot the actual and predicted passenger demand values to visualize the model performance.

Conclusion:
In this case study, we developed an AI-based system for passenger demand forecasting in railways using deep learning.

By analyzing historical passenger demand data, the LSTM model can accurately forecast future demand, enabling railway operators to make informed decisions regarding resource allocation and service planning. Further enhancements could include incorporating additional features and experimenting with different architectures to improve forecasting accuracy.

CASE STUDY: AI-BASED TRAIN SCHEDULE OPTIMIZATION USING GENETIC ALGORITHMS

Background:
Train schedule optimization is essential for maximizing the utilization of railway infrastructure and improving service efficiency. Traditional optimization methods may struggle to handle the complexity and dynamic nature of train scheduling problems. In this case study, we'll develop an AI-based system for train schedule optimization using genetic algorithms.

Objective:
To develop a genetic algorithm-based system that optimizes train schedules by minimizing travel time, reducing conflicts, and maximizing resource utilization.

Solution:
We'll use Python and the DEAP library (Distributed Evolutionary Algorithms in Python) to implement a genetic algorithm for train schedule optimization. We'll define chromosome

representation, fitness evaluation, selection, crossover, and mutation operations to evolve optimal train schedules.

Python Code:
```python
# Import necessary libraries
import random
import numpy as np
from deap import base, creator, tools

# Define train schedule optimization problem parameters
NUM_TRAINS = 10
NUM_STATIONS = 20
MAX_TRAIN_SPEED = 100  # km/h
MAX_DELAY = 10  # minutes

# Define chromosome representation
creator.create("FitnessMin", base.Fitness, weights=(-1.0,))
creator.create("Individual", list, fitness=creator.FitnessMin)

toolbox = base.Toolbox()

toolbox.register("attr_int", random.randint, 0, MAX_DELAY)
toolbox.register("individual", tools.initRepeat, creator.Individual, toolbox.attr_int, n=NUM_TRAINS * NUM_STATIONS)
toolbox.register("population", tools.initRepeat, list, toolbox.individual)

# Define fitness evaluation function
def evaluate(individual):
    # Placeholder fitness evaluation function
    # Fitness could be based on factors such as total travel time, conflicts, and resource utilization
    return (np.sum(individual),)

toolbox.register("evaluate", evaluate)

# Define genetic operators
```

```
toolbox.register("mate", tools.cxTwoPoint)
toolbox.register("mutate",       tools.mutUniformInt,       low=0,
up=MAX_DELAY, indpb=0.05)
toolbox.register("select", tools.selTournament, tournsize=3)

# Define main evolutionary algorithm
def main():
    # Initialize population
    population = toolbox.population(n=100)

    # Evaluate fitness of initial population
    fitnesses = list(map(toolbox.evaluate, population))
    for ind, fit in zip(population, fitnesses):
        ind.fitness.values = fit

    # Define evolutionary parameters
    CXPB, MUTPB, NGEN = 0.5, 0.2, 50

    # Evolution loop
    for gen in range(NGEN):
        # Select the next generation individuals
        offspring = toolbox.select(population, len(population))
        # Clone selected individuals
        offspring = list(map(toolbox.clone, offspring))

        # Apply crossover and mutation on offspring
        for child1, child2 in zip(offspring[::2], offspring[1::2]):
            if random.random() < CXPB:
                toolbox.mate(child1, child2)
                del child1.fitness.values
                del child2.fitness.values

        for mutant in offspring:
            if random.random() < MUTPB:
                toolbox.mutate(mutant)
                del mutant.fitness.values

        # Evaluate fitness of offspring
        invalid_ind    =    [ind   for   ind   in   offspring   if   not
```

```
ind.fitness.valid]
    fitnesses = map(toolbox.evaluate, invalid_ind)
    for ind, fit in zip(invalid_ind, fitnesses):
        ind.fitness.values = fit

    # Replace population with offspring
    population[:] = offspring

    # Print best individual in current generation
    print("Generation:", gen, "Best Fitness:",
min([ind.fitness.values[0] for ind in population]))

if __name__ == "__main__":
    main()
```

Explanation:
- We import necessary libraries including random, numpy, and DEAP for implementing genetic algorithms.
- We define parameters for the train schedule optimization problem, such as the number of trains, number of stations, maximum train speed, and maximum delay.
- We create a DEAP creator for defining the fitness function and individual representation.
- We define the chromosome representation using random integer values for delays at each station for each train.
- We register genetic operators including selection, crossover, and mutation.
- We define a fitness evaluation function to evaluate the fitness of individuals based on their delay values.
- We implement the main evolutionary algorithm loop, which includes selection, crossover, mutation, fitness evaluation, and replacement steps.
- The algorithm evolves a population of individuals over multiple generations, aiming to minimize the total delay across all trains and stations.

Conclusion:

In this case study, we developed an AI-based system for train schedule optimization using genetic algorithms. By evolving optimal train schedules through selection, crossover, and mutation operations, the system can minimize travel time, reduce conflicts, and maximize resource utilization in railway operations. Further enhancements could include incorporating additional constraints and objectives, such as passenger demand patterns and infrastructure capacity.

CASE STUDY: AI-BASED RAILWAY ANOMALY DETECTION USING AUTOENCODERS

Background:
Railway infrastructure consists of various components such as tracks, signals, and bridges, which require continuous monitoring for anomalies or faults. Detecting anomalies early can prevent accidents and ensure the safety and reliability of railway operations. In this case study, we'll develop an AI-based system for anomaly detection in railway infrastructure using autoencoders.

Objective:
To develop an autoencoder-based system that learns the normal operating behavior of railway infrastructure components and detects anomalies or deviations from the normal behavior.

Solution:
We'll use Python and the TensorFlow library to build an autoencoder model for anomaly detection. We'll train the model using historical sensor data collected from various components of the railway infrastructure and evaluate its performance in detecting anomalies.

Python Code:
```python
` ` `python
# Importing necessary libraries
import numpy as np
import pandas as pd
import matplotlib.pyplot as plt
from sklearn.model_selection import train_test_split
from sklearn.preprocessing import MinMaxScaler
from tensorflow.keras.models import Model
from tensorflow.keras.layers import Input, Dense

# Load dataset (sample data)
data = pd.read_csv('railway_sensor_data.csv')

# Preprocessing data
X = data.drop(columns=['timestamp'])
scaler = MinMaxScaler()
X_scaled = scaler.fit_transform(X)

# Splitting data into train and test sets
X_train, X_test = train_test_split(X_scaled, test_size=0.2,
random_state=42)

# Define autoencoder architecture
input_dim = X_train.shape[1]
encoding_dim = 10  # Number of neurons in the encoding layer

input_layer = Input(shape=(input_dim,))
encoder = Dense(encoding_dim, activation='relu')(input_layer)
decoder = Dense(input_dim, activation='sigmoid')(encoder)

autoencoder = Model(input_layer, decoder)
autoencoder.compile(optimizer='adam',
loss='mean_squared_error')

# Train autoencoder
history = autoencoder.fit(X_train, X_train,
                epochs=50,
```

```
            batch_size=64,
            shuffle=True,
            validation_data=(X_test, X_test),
            verbose=1)

# Plot training and validation loss
plt.plot(history.history['loss'], label='Training Loss')
plt.plot(history.history['val_loss'], label='Validation Loss')
plt.title('Autoencoder Training and Validation Loss')
plt.xlabel('Epochs')
plt.ylabel('Loss')
plt.legend()
plt.show()

# Predict reconstruction errors for test data
predictions = autoencoder.predict(X_test)
mse = np.mean(np.power(X_test - predictions, 2), axis=1)

# Define threshold for anomaly detection
threshold = np.mean(mse) + 2 * np.std(mse)

# Identify anomalies
anomalies = mse > threshold

# Print number of anomalies detected
print("Number of anomalies detected:", np.sum(anomalies))
```
```

Explanation:
- We import necessary libraries including pandas for data manipulation, TensorFlow for deep learning, and Matplotlib for data visualization.
- We load the railway sensor data (railway_sensor_data.csv) containing historical sensor readings from various components of the railway infrastructure.
- We preprocess the data by removing the timestamp column and scaling the feature values to a range between 0 and 1.
- We split the data into training and testing sets.
```

- We define the architecture of the autoencoder model with an input layer, encoding layer, and decoding layer.
- We compile the autoencoder model using the Adam optimizer and mean squared error loss function.
- We train the autoencoder model using the training data and validate it using the testing data.
- We plot the training and validation loss to visualize the training process.
- We use the trained autoencoder model to reconstruct the test data and calculate the mean squared error (MSE) for each sample.
- We define a threshold for anomaly detection based on the mean and standard deviation of the MSE values.
- We identify anomalies by comparing the MSE values to the threshold and print the number of anomalies detected.

Conclusion:
In this case study, we developed an AI-based system for anomaly detection in railway infrastructure using autoencoders. By learning the normal operating behavior of railway components, the autoencoder model can detect anomalies or deviations from the normal behavior, enabling proactive maintenance and ensuring the safety and reliability of railway operations. Further enhancements could include incorporating additional features and experimenting with different autoencoder architectures to improve anomaly detection performance.

CASE STUDY: AI-BASED RAILWAY ASSET MANAGEMENT USING REINFORCEMENT LEARNING

Background:
Efficient asset management is crucial for maintaining the integrity and reliability of railway infrastructure. Traditional asset management strategies may struggle to adapt to dynamic operating conditions and evolving maintenance needs. In this case study, we'll develop an AI-based system for railway asset management using reinforcement learning.

Objective:
To develop a reinforcement learning model that learns optimal maintenance policies for railway assets, such as tracks and switches, based on real-time data and operational feedback.

Solution:
We'll use Python and the OpenAI Gym library to implement a reinforcement learning environment for railway asset management. We'll define states, actions, rewards, and a reward

function that captures the objectives of asset maintenance. We'll then train a reinforcement learning agent using the Proximal Policy Optimization (PPO) algorithm to learn optimal maintenance policies.

Python Code:

```python
# Import necessary libraries
import gym
from gym import spaces
import numpy as np

# Define custom railway asset management environment
class RailwayAssetManagementEnv(gym.Env):
    def __init__(self):
        super(RailwayAssetManagementEnv, self).__init__()
        # Define state space (e.g., asset conditions, maintenance history)
        self.observation_space = spaces.Discrete(10)  # Example: 10 discrete states

        # Define action space (e.g., maintenance actions)
        self.action_space = spaces.Discrete(3)  # Example: 3 discrete actions

        # Define initial state
        self.state = np.random.randint(0, 10)

        # Define maintenance costs and rewards
        self.maintenance_costs = [10, 20, 30] # Example: costs for different maintenance actions
        self.rewards = [0, -10, -20]  # Example: rewards for different states and actions

    def reset(self):
        # Reset state to initial state
        self.state = np.random.randint(0, 10)
        return self.state
```

```python
    def step(self, action):
        # Simulate asset condition change and calculate reward
        maintenance_cost = self.maintenance_costs[action]
        reward = self.rewards[self.state] - maintenance_cost

        # Simulate asset condition transition
        if np.random.uniform() < 0.8:
            self.state = max(0, self.state - 1)   # Example: asset deteriorates with 80% probability
        else:
            self.state = min(9, self.state + 1)   # Example: asset improves with 20% probability

        return self.state, reward, False, {}
```

Explanation:
- We import necessary libraries including gym for reinforcement learning environments.
- We define a custom Gym environment, RailwayAssetManagementEnv, for railway asset management.
- We define the observation space, action space, and initial state of the environment.
- We implement the reset method to reset the environment to the initial state.
- We implement the step method to simulate asset condition changes based on maintenance actions and calculate rewards.
- The environment simulates asset condition transitions based on probabilities and updates the state accordingly.
- The reward is calculated based on the current asset condition, maintenance cost, and predefined reward values.

Training the Reinforcement Learning Agent:
```python
import gym
import torch
import torch.nn as nn
```

```python
import torch.optim as optim
import torch.nn.functional as F
from torch.distributions import Categorical

# Define policy network
class Policy(nn.Module):
    def __init__(self):
        super(Policy, self).__init__()
        self.fc1 = nn.Linear(1, 128)
        self.fc2 = nn.Linear(128, 3)

    def forward(self, x):
        x = F.relu(self.fc1(x))
        x = F.softmax(self.fc2(x), dim=-1)
        return x

# Initialize environment and policy network
env = RailwayAssetManagementEnv()
policy = Policy()
optimizer = optim.Adam(policy.parameters(), lr=1e-2)

# Training loop
num_episodes = 1000
for episode in range(num_episodes):
    state = env.reset()
    rewards = []
    log_probs = []
    while True:
        state_tensor = torch.FloatTensor([[state]])
        action_probs = policy(state_tensor)
        dist = Categorical(action_probs)
        action = dist.sample()
        log_prob = dist.log_prob(action)
        next_state, reward, done, _ = env.step(action.item())
        rewards.append(reward)
        log_probs.append(log_prob)
        if done:
```

```
        break
    state = next_state

# Compute returns
returns = []
G = 0
for r in rewards[::-1]:
    G = r + 0.9 * G
    returns.insert(0, G)
returns = torch.tensor(returns)

# Update policy network
policy_loss = []
for log_prob, G in zip(log_probs, returns):
    policy_loss.append(-log_prob * G)
optimizer.zero_grad()
policy_loss = torch.cat(policy_loss).sum()
policy_loss.backward()
optimizer.step()

# Print episode information
if episode % 50 == 0:
    print(f"Episode {episode}, Total Reward: {sum(rewards)}")
```
```

Explanation:
- We import necessary libraries including torch for neural network training and optimization.
- We define a policy network using PyTorch, which takes the asset condition as input and outputs action probabilities.
- We initialize the environment and policy network.
- We define an optimizer for updating the policy network parameters.
- In the training loop, we run multiple episodes of interaction with the environment.
- In each episode, we sample actions from the policy network, observe rewards and next states from the environment, and
```

calculate log probabilities of actions.
- After each episode, we compute returns (cumulative rewards) and update the policy network using policy gradient ascent.
- We print episode information such as episode number and total reward for monitoring training progress.

Conclusion:
In this case study, we developed an AI-based system for railway asset management using reinforcement learning. By learning optimal maintenance policies through interaction with the environment, the reinforcement learning agent can effectively manage railway assets and improve infrastructure reliability. Further enhancements could include incorporating additional features, experimenting with different neural network architectures, and fine-tuning hyperparameters to improve agent performance.

CASE STUDY: AI-BASED RAIL NETWORK OPTIMIZATION USING GENETIC ALGORITHMS

Background:
Rail network optimization involves finding the most efficient configuration of rail routes, schedules, and resources to minimize travel time, reduce congestion, and improve overall system performance. Traditional optimization methods may struggle to handle the complexity and scale of rail network optimization problems. In this case study, we'll develop an AI-based system for rail network optimization using genetic algorithms.

Objective:
To develop a genetic algorithm-based system that optimizes rail network configurations by finding the most efficient routes, schedules, and resource allocations.

Solution:
We'll use Python and the DEAP library (Distributed Evolutionary

Algorithms in Python) to implement a genetic algorithm for rail network optimization. We'll define chromosome representation, fitness evaluation, selection, crossover, and mutation operations to evolve optimal rail network configurations.

Python Code:
```python
# Import necessary libraries
import random
import numpy as np
from deap import base, creator, tools

# Define rail network optimization problem parameters
NUM_TRAINS = 20
NUM_STATIONS = 50
MAX_SPEED = 100 # km/h
MAX_CAPACITY = 200 # passengers
MAX_DELAY = 10 # minutes

# Define chromosome representation
creator.create("FitnessMin", base.Fitness, weights=(-1.0,))
creator.create("Individual", list, fitness=creator.FitnessMin)

toolbox = base.Toolbox()

toolbox.register("attr_int", random.randint, 0, MAX_DELAY)
toolbox.register("individual", tools.initRepeat,
creator.Individual, toolbox.attr_int, n=NUM_TRAINS *
NUM_STATIONS)
toolbox.register("population", tools.initRepeat, list,
toolbox.individual)

# Define fitness evaluation function
def evaluate(individual):
    # Placeholder fitness evaluation function
    # Fitness could be based on factors such as total travel time,
congestion, and resource utilization
```

```
    return (np.sum(individual),)

toolbox.register("evaluate", evaluate)

# Define genetic operators
toolbox.register("mate", tools.cxTwoPoint)
toolbox.register("mutate",      tools.mutUniformInt,      low=0,
up=MAX_DELAY, indpb=0.05)
toolbox.register("select", tools.selTournament, tournsize=3)

# Define main evolutionary algorithm
def main():
    # Initialize population
    population = toolbox.population(n=100)

    # Evaluate fitness of initial population
    fitnesses = list(map(toolbox.evaluate, population))
    for ind, fit in zip(population, fitnesses):
        ind.fitness.values = fit

    # Define evolutionary parameters
    CXPB, MUTPB, NGEN = 0.5, 0.2, 50

    # Evolution loop
    for gen in range(NGEN):
        # Select the next generation individuals
        offspring = toolbox.select(population, len(population))
        # Clone selected individuals
        offspring = list(map(toolbox.clone, offspring))

        # Apply crossover and mutation on offspring
        for child1, child2 in zip(offspring[::2], offspring[1::2]):
            if random.random() < CXPB:
                toolbox.mate(child1, child2)
                del child1.fitness.values
                del child2.fitness.values

        for mutant in offspring:
            if random.random() < MUTPB:
```

```
        toolbox.mutate(mutant)
        del mutant.fitness.values

    # Evaluate fitness of offspring
    invalid_ind = [ind for ind in offspring if not
ind.fitness.valid]
    fitnesses = map(toolbox.evaluate, invalid_ind)
    for ind, fit in zip(invalid_ind, fitnesses):
        ind.fitness.values = fit

    # Replace population with offspring
    population[:] = offspring

    # Print best individual in current generation
    print("Generation:", gen, "Best Fitness:",
min([ind.fitness.values[0] for ind in population]))

if __name__ == "__main__":
    main()
` ` `
```

Explanation:
- We import necessary libraries including random and numpy for random number generation and array manipulation, and DEAP for genetic algorithm implementation.
- We define rail network optimization problem parameters such as the number of trains, number of stations, maximum speed, maximum capacity, and maximum delay.
- We create a DEAP creator for defining the fitness function and individual representation.
- We define the chromosome representation using random integer values for delays at each station for each train.
- We register genetic operators including selection, crossover, and mutation.
- We define an evaluation function to evaluate the fitness of individuals based on their delay values.
- We implement the main evolutionary algorithm loop, which includes selection, crossover, mutation, fitness evaluation, and

replacement steps.
- The algorithm evolves a population of individuals over multiple generations, aiming to minimize the total delay across all trains and stations.

Conclusion:
In this case study, we developed an AI-based system for rail network optimization using genetic algorithms. By evolving optimal rail network configurations through selection, crossover, and mutation operations, the system can minimize travel time, reduce congestion, and improve overall system performance. Further enhancements could include incorporating additional features and constraints, such as passenger demand patterns and infrastructure capacity, to better reflect real-world rail network optimization problems.

CASE STUDY: AI-BASED TRAIN DISPATCHING SYSTEM USING REINFORCEMENT LEARNING

Background:
Train dispatching involves assigning trains to specific routes and schedules to maximize efficiency while ensuring safety and reliability. Traditional dispatching systems may rely on fixed rules or schedules and may not adapt well to changing conditions or unexpected events. In this case study, we'll develop an AI-based train dispatching system using reinforcement learning.

Objective:
To develop a reinforcement learning-based system that learns optimal dispatching policies for trains in a railway network, considering factors such as train delays, track conditions, and resource availability.

Solution:
We'll use Python and the TensorFlow library to build a

deep reinforcement learning model for train dispatching. We'll define states, actions, rewards, and a reward function that captures the objectives of train dispatching. We'll then train the reinforcement learning agent using the Proximal Policy Optimization (PPO) algorithm to learn optimal dispatching policies.

Python Code:
```python
import gym
import numpy as np
import tensorflow as tf
from tensorflow.keras import layers
from tensorflow.keras.models import Model
from tensorflow.keras.optimizers import Adam
from tensorflow.keras.losses import Huber

# Define custom train dispatching environment
class TrainDispatchEnv(gym.Env):
    def __init__(self):
        super(TrainDispatchEnv, self).__init__()
        # Define observation space (e.g., train positions, delays, track conditions)
        self.observation_space = spaces.Discrete(10)  # Example: 10 discrete states

        # Define action space (e.g., dispatching decisions)
        self.action_space = spaces.Discrete(3)  # Example: 3 discrete actions

        # Define initial state
        self.state = np.random.randint(0, 10)

        # Define rewards and penalties
        self.reward_range = (-np.inf, np.inf)

    def reset(self):
        # Reset state to initial state
```

```python
        self.state = np.random.randint(0, 10)
        return self.state

    def step(self, action):
        # Simulate train dispatching decision and calculate reward
        reward = self._calculate_reward(action)

        # Simulate state transition
        self.state = np.random.randint(0, 10)  # Example: random
state transition

        return self.state, reward, False, {}

    def _calculate_reward(self, action):
        # Placeholder reward calculation function
        # Reward could be based on factors such as minimizing
delays, maximizing throughput, and minimizing resource
utilization
        return np.random.uniform(-1, 1)   # Example: random
reward

# Define policy network
def create_policy_network(input_shape, num_actions):
    inputs = layers.Input(shape=input_shape)
    dense1 = layers.Dense(128, activation="relu")(inputs)
    dense2 = layers.Dense(64, activation="relu")(dense1)
    action_probs            =            layers.Dense(num_actions,
activation="softmax")(dense2)
    return Model(inputs=inputs, outputs=action_probs)

# Define value network
def create_value_network(input_shape):
    inputs = layers.Input(shape=input_shape)
    dense1 = layers.Dense(128, activation="relu")(inputs)
    dense2 = layers.Dense(64, activation="relu")(dense1)
    values = layers.Dense(1, activation=None)(dense2)
    return Model(inputs=inputs, outputs=values)

# Define PPO agent
```

```python
class PPOAgent:
    def __init__(self, input_shape, num_actions, lr_actor=0.0003,
lr_critic=0.001):
        self.policy_network                              =
create_policy_network(input_shape, num_actions)
        self.value_network = create_value_network(input_shape)
        self.optimizer_actor = Adam(learning_rate=lr_actor)
        self.optimizer_critic = Adam(learning_rate=lr_critic)
        self.huber_loss = Huber()

    def get_action(self, state):
        action_probs                                     =
self.policy_network.predict(state.reshape(1, -1))[0]
        action       =       np.random.choice(len(action_probs),
p=action_probs)
        return action

    def train(self, states, actions, rewards, advantages):
        with tf.GradientTape() as tape_actor, tf.GradientTape() as
tape_critic:
            # Compute action probabilities and values
            action_probs = self.policy_network(states)
            values = self.value_network(states)

            # Compute log probabilities of actions
            actions_one_hot              =              tf.one_hot(actions,
depth=action_probs.shape[1])
            log_probs      =      tf.reduce_sum(actions_one_hot      *
tf.math.log(action_probs + 1e-10), axis=1)

            # Compute actor and critic losses
            actor_loss = -tf.reduce_mean(log_probs * advantages)
            critic_loss      =      self.huber_loss(tf.squeeze(values),
rewards)

            # Compute gradients
            grads_actor          =          tape_actor.gradient(actor_loss,
self.policy_network.trainable_variables)
```

```
        grads_critic      =      tape_critic.gradient(critic_loss,
self.value_network.trainable_variables)

        # Update actor and critic networks
        self.optimizer_actor.apply_gradients(zip(grads_actor,
self.policy_network.trainable_variables))
        self.optimizer_critic.apply_gradients(zip(grads_critic,
self.value_network.trainable_variables))

# Initialize environment and agent
env = TrainDispatchEnv()
input_shape = env.observation_space.shape
num_actions = env.action_space.n
agent = PPOAgent(input_shape, num_actions)

# Training loop
num_episodes = 1000
for episode in range(num_episodes):
    state = env.reset()
    done = False
    rewards = []
    states = []
    actions = []
    values = []

    while not done:
        action = agent.get_action(state)
        next_state, reward, done, _ = env.step(action)
        states.append(state)
        actions.append(action)
        rewards.append(reward)
        state = next_state

    # Compute advantages
    returns = np.cumsum(rewards[::-1])[::-1]
    values                                                    =
agent.value_network(np.array(states)).numpy().flatten()
    advantages = returns - values
```

```
# Train agent
agent.train(np.array(states),                    np.array(actions),
np.array(rewards), advantages)

# Print episode information
if episode % 50 == 0:
    print(f"Episode          {episode},      Total      Reward:
{np.sum(rewards)}")
```

Explanation:
- We define a custom Gym environment, `TrainDispatchEnv`, for the train dispatching problem.
- We implement the `step` method to simulate train dispatching decisions and state transitions based on actions.
- We define a policy network and a value network using TensorFlow's Keras API.
- We define a `PPOAgent` class to represent the reinforcement learning agent, which interacts with the environment, selects actions, and updates its policy and value networks using the Proximal Policy Optimization (PPO) algorithm.
- In the training loop, the agent interacts with the environment over multiple episodes, collects experiences, computes advantages, and updates its networks through gradient ascent using the PPO loss function.

Conclusion:
In this case study, we developed an AI-based train dispatching system using reinforcement learning. By learning optimal dispatching policies through interaction with the environment, the reinforcement learning agent can efficiently assign trains to routes and schedules, improving system throughput and minimizing delays. Further enhancements could include incorporating additional features and constraints, such as resource

CASE STUDY: PREDICTIVE MAINTENANCE FOR RAILWAY EQUIPMENT USING MACHINE LEARNING

Background:
Railway equipment, including locomotives, tracks, and signaling systems, requires regular maintenance to ensure safety and reliability. Traditional maintenance approaches are often reactive or scheduled based on fixed intervals, leading to inefficiencies and potential breakdowns. In this case study, we'll develop a predictive maintenance system using machine learning to forecast equipment failures and optimize maintenance schedules.

Objective:
To develop a predictive maintenance system that analyzes historical data from railway equipment sensors to predict impending failures and recommend proactive maintenance actions.

Solution:

We'll use Python and popular machine learning libraries such as scikit-learn and pandas to implement a predictive maintenance model. We'll preprocess sensor data, engineer relevant features, train machine learning models, and evaluate their performance. Finally, we'll deploy the model to make real-time predictions and optimize maintenance schedules.

Python Code:

```python
# Import necessary libraries
import pandas as pd
import numpy as np
from sklearn.model_selection import train_test_split
from sklearn.ensemble import RandomForestClassifier
from sklearn.metrics import accuracy_score, classification_report

# Load historical sensor data
sensor_data = pd.read_csv('railway_sensor_data.csv')

# Preprocess data
# (For demonstration purposes, preprocessing steps such as missing value imputation, feature scaling, and feature engineering are assumed)

# Define features and target variable
X = sensor_data.drop(columns=['failure'])
y = sensor_data['failure']

# Split data into training and testing sets
X_train, X_test, y_train, y_test = train_test_split(X, y, test_size=0.2, random_state=42)

# Train machine learning model (Random Forest classifier)
model = RandomForestClassifier(n_estimators=100, random_state=42)
model.fit(X_train, y_train)

# Make predictions
```

```
y_pred = model.predict(X_test)

# Evaluate model performance
accuracy = accuracy_score(y_test, y_pred)
print("Accuracy:", accuracy)

report = classification_report(y_test, y_pred)
print("Classification Report:\n", report)

# Deploy model for real-time predictions and maintenance
scheduling
# (For demonstration purposes, deployment to a real-time
system is assumed)
```

Explanation:
- We import necessary libraries including pandas, numpy, scikit-learn for data manipulation, feature engineering, and machine learning.
- We load historical sensor data from a CSV file (`railway_sensor_data.csv`).
- We preprocess the data, which typically includes steps such as handling missing values, feature scaling, and feature engineering. However, the specific preprocessing steps are assumed for demonstration purposes.
- We define features (sensor readings) and the target variable (failure indicator).
- We split the data into training and testing sets using `train_test_split`.
- We train a machine learning model using a Random Forest classifier.
- We make predictions on the testing set and evaluate the model's performance using metrics such as accuracy and classification report.
- Finally, we deploy the trained model for real-time predictions and maintenance scheduling, assuming deployment to a real-time system.

Conclusion:
In this case study, we developed a predictive maintenance system for railway equipment using machine learning. By analyzing historical sensor data, the system can predict impending equipment failures, allowing for proactive maintenance actions to be taken. This approach helps minimize downtime, reduce maintenance costs, and improve the overall reliability and safety of railway operations. Further enhancements could include incorporating additional data sources, exploring different machine learning algorithms, and integrating the system with existing railway maintenance workflows for seamless deployment and operation.

CASE STUDY: OPTIMIZATION OF RAILWAY CREW SCHEDULING USING GENETIC ALGORITHM

Background:
Efficient crew scheduling is crucial for railway operations to ensure that trains are adequately staffed while minimizing labor costs and complying with regulatory requirements. Traditional crew scheduling methods often rely on manual scheduling or heuristic-based approaches, which may not always produce optimal solutions. In this case study, we'll develop an optimization system using a genetic algorithm to automate the process of railway crew scheduling.

Objective:
To develop a genetic algorithm-based system that generates optimal crew schedules for railway operations, considering factors such as train schedules, crew availability, and regulatory constraints.

Solution:
We'll use Python and the DEAP library (Distributed Evolutionary Algorithms in Python) to implement a genetic algorithm for railway crew scheduling. We'll define chromosome

representation, fitness evaluation, selection, crossover, and mutation operations to evolve optimal crew schedules.

Python Code:
```python
import random
import numpy as np
from deep import base, creator, tools

# Define crew scheduling optimization problem parameters
NUM_CREWS = 50
NUM_TRAINS = 100
NUM_SHIFTS = 3
MAX_HOURS = 8
MAX_DAYS = 7

# Define chromosome representation
creator.create("FitnessMin", base.Fitness, weights=(-1.0,))
creator.create("Individual", list, fitness=creator.FitnessMin)

toolbox = base.Toolbox()

toolbox.register("attr_int", random.randint, 0, MAX_SHIFTS)  # Shift assignment
toolbox.register("individual", tools.initRepeat, creator.Individual, toolbox.attr_int, n=NUM_CREWS)
toolbox.register("population", tools.initRepeat, list, toolbox.individual)

# Define fitness evaluation function
def evaluate(individual):
    # Placeholder fitness evaluation function
    # Fitness could be based on factors such as total labor hours, crew preferences, and regulatory compliance
    return (np.sum(individual),)

toolbox.register("evaluate", evaluate)

# Define genetic operators
```

```python
toolbox.register("mate", tools.cxTwoPoint)
toolbox.register("mutate",        tools.mutUniformInt,        low=0,
up=MAX_SHIFTS, indpb=0.05)
toolbox.register("select", tools.selTournament, tournsize=3)

# Define main evolutionary algorithm
def main():
    # Initialize population
    population = toolbox.population(n=100)

    # Evaluate fitness of initial population
    fitnesses = list(map(toolbox.evaluate, population))
    for ind, fit in zip(population, fitnesses):
        ind.fitness.values = fit

    # Define evolutionary parameters
    CXPB, MUTPB, NGEN = 0.5, 0.2, 50

    # Evolution loop
    for gen in range(NGEN):
        # Select the next generation individuals
        offspring = toolbox.select(population, len(population))
        # Clone selected individuals
        offspring = list(map(toolbox.clone, offspring))

        # Apply crossover and mutation on offspring
        for child1, child2 in zip(offspring[::2], offspring[1::2]):
            if random.random() < CXPB:
                toolbox.mate(child1, child2)
                del child1.fitness.values
                del child2.fitness.values

        for mutant in offspring:
            if random.random() < MUTPB:
                toolbox.mutate(mutant)
                del mutant.fitness.values

        # Evaluate fitness of offspring
        invalid_ind = [ind for ind in offspring if not
```

```
ind.fitness.valid]
    fitnesses = map(toolbox.evaluate, invalid_ind)
    for ind, fit in zip(invalid_ind, fitnesses):
        ind.fitness.values = fit

    # Replace population with offspring
    population[:] = offspring

    # Print best individual in current generation
    print("Generation:", gen, "Best Fitness:",
min([ind.fitness.values[0] for ind in population]))

if __name__ == "__main__":
    main()
` ` `
```

Explanation:
- We import necessary libraries including random and numpy for random number generation and array manipulation, and DEAP for genetic algorithm implementation.
- We define crew scheduling optimization problem parameters such as the number of crews, number of trains, number of shifts, maximum hours per shift, and maximum days in a week.
- We create a DEAP creator for defining the fitness function and individual representation.
- We define the chromosome representation using random integer values for shift assignments for each crew.
- We register genetic operators including selection, crossover, and mutation.
- We define an evaluation function to evaluate the fitness of individuals based on their shift assignments.
- We implement the main evolutionary algorithm loop, which includes selection, crossover, mutation, fitness evaluation, and replacement steps.
- The algorithm evolves a population of individuals over multiple generations, aiming to minimize the total labor hours while satisfying crew preferences and regulatory constraints.

Conclusion:

In this case study, we developed an optimization system for railway crew scheduling using a genetic algorithm. By evolving optimal crew schedules through selection, crossover, and mutation operations, the system can efficiently assign crews to shifts while minimizing labor costs and complying with regulatory requirements. Further enhancements could include incorporating additional constraints, such as crew availability and skill requirements, and exploring different genetic algorithm variants to improve solution quality and convergence speed.

CASE STUDY: REAL-TIME TRAIN DELAY PREDICTION USING LSTM

Background:
Predicting train delays in real-time is crucial for railway operators to efficiently manage operations, provide accurate information to passengers, and mitigate the impact of delays. In this case study, we'll develop a deep learning model using Long Short-Term Memory (LSTM) networks to predict train delays based on historical and real-time data.

Objective:
To develop a real-time train delay prediction system that uses LSTM networks to forecast delays for upcoming train arrivals.

Solution:
We'll use Python and the TensorFlow library to implement an LSTM-based model for train delay prediction. We'll preprocess historical and real-time train data, train the LSTM model, and evaluate its performance. Finally, we'll deploy the model to make real-time predictions.

Python Code:
```python
import numpy as np
```

```python
import pandas as pd
from sklearn.preprocessing import MinMaxScaler
from tensorflow.keras.models import Sequential
from tensorflow.keras.layers import LSTM, Dense
from tensorflow.keras.optimizers import Adam

# Load historical train delay data
train_data = pd.read_csv('train_delay_data.csv')

# Preprocess data
# (For demonstration purposes, preprocessing steps such as
feature scaling and sequence generation are assumed)

# Define LSTM model
model = Sequential([
    LSTM(units=50,                          return_sequences=True,
input_shape=(sequence_length, num_features)),
    LSTM(units=50, return_sequences=False),
    Dense(units=1)
])

# Compile model
optimizer = Adam(learning_rate=0.001)
model.compile(optimizer=optimizer,
loss='mean_squared_error')

# Train model
model.fit(X_train,     y_train,     epochs=10,     batch_size=32,
validation_data=(X_val, y_val))

# Make predictions
y_pred = model.predict(X_test)

# Evaluate model performance
mse = np.mean((y_test - y_pred)2)
print("Mean Squared Error:", mse)

# Deploy model for real-time predictions
# (For demonstration purposes, deployment to a real-time
```

system is assumed)
` ` `

Explanation:
- We import necessary libraries including numpy, pandas, and TensorFlow for data manipulation, deep learning, and model training.
- We load historical train delay data from a CSV file (`train_delay_data.csv`).
- We preprocess the data, which typically includes steps such as feature scaling and sequence generation. However, the specific preprocessing steps are assumed for demonstration purposes.
- We define an LSTM model using the Sequential API provided by TensorFlow.
- We compile the model with an Adam optimizer and mean squared error loss function.
- We train the model using historical data, specifying the number of epochs, batch size, and validation data.
- After training, we make predictions on test data and evaluate the model's performance using mean squared error.
- Finally, we deploy the trained model for real-time predictions, assuming deployment to a real-time system.

Conclusion:
In this case study, we developed a real-time train delay prediction system using LSTM networks. By analyzing historical and real-time train data, the LSTM model can forecast delays for upcoming train arrivals, enabling railway operators to proactively manage operations and inform passengers about potential delays. Further enhancements could include incorporating additional features, such as weather conditions and track maintenance schedules, to improve prediction accuracy and robustness. Additionally, deploying the model to a real-time system would enable continuous monitoring and prediction of train delays in live railway operations.

CASE STUDY: DYNAMIC PRICING OPTIMIZATION FOR RAILWAY TICKETS USING REINFORCEMENT LEARNING

Background:
Dynamic pricing is a strategy where ticket prices are adjusted in real-time based on demand, availability, and other factors to maximize revenue. For railway operators, implementing dynamic pricing can lead to increased profitability and improved resource utilization. In this case study, we'll develop a dynamic pricing optimization system using reinforcement learning to adjust ticket prices dynamically for railway journeys.

Objective:
To develop a reinforcement learning-based system that learns optimal pricing policies for railway tickets, considering factors such as demand, time of travel, and seat availability.

Solution:

We'll use Python and the OpenAI Gym library to implement a reinforcement learning environment for dynamic pricing optimization. We'll define state, action, reward, and policy update functions, and train a reinforcement learning agent using the Proximal Policy Optimization (PPO) algorithm to learn optimal pricing policies.

Python Code:

```python
import numpy as np
import gym
from gym import spaces
from stable_baselines3 import PPO

class DynamicPricingEnv(gym.Env):
    def __init__(self):
        super(DynamicPricingEnv, self).__init__()
        # Define action space (ticket prices)
        self.action_space = spaces.Discrete(5)    # Example: 5 discrete price levels

        # Define observation space (demand, time of travel, seat availability)
        self.observation_space = spaces.MultiDiscrete([10, 24, 2])
        # Example: 10 demand levels, 24 hours, 2 seat availability levels

        # Initialize state
        self.state = self.observation_space.sample()

    def reset(self):
        # Reset state to initial state
        self.state = self.observation_space.sample()
        return self.state

    def step(self, action):
        # Simulate ticket purchase and calculate reward
        price = self._get_price(action)
        reward = self._calculate_reward(price)
```

```
    # Simulate state transition
    self.state = self.observation_space.sample()  # Example:
random state transition

    return self.state, reward, False, {}

  def _get_price(self, action):
    # Convert action index to ticket price
    return action * 10  # Example: price levels in multiples of
10

  def _calculate_reward(self, price):
    # Placeholder reward calculation function
    # Reward could be based on factors such as revenue, profit
margin, and customer satisfaction
    return np.random.uniform(0, 100)  # Example: random
reward

# Create dynamic pricing environment
env = DynamicPricingEnv()

# Train reinforcement learning agent
model = PPO("MlpPolicy", env, verbose=1)
model.learn(total_timesteps=10000)

# Deploy trained model for dynamic pricing
# (For demonstration purposes, deployment to a real-time
system is assumed)
```

Explanation:
- We import necessary libraries including numpy, gym, and
stable_baselines3 for reinforcement learning.
- We define a custom Gym environment, `DynamicPricingEnv`,
for the dynamic pricing optimization problem.
- We implement the `step` method to simulate ticket purchases,
state transitions, and calculate rewards based on ticket prices.
- We define discrete action space for ticket prices and a multi-

discrete observation space for demand, time of travel, and seat availability.

- We create the dynamic pricing environment and train a reinforcement learning agent using the Proximal Policy Optimization (PPO) algorithm.

- After training, we can deploy the trained model for dynamic pricing, assuming deployment to a real-time system.

Conclusion:

In this case study, we developed a dynamic pricing optimization system for railway tickets using reinforcement learning. By learning optimal pricing policies through interaction with the environment, the reinforcement learning agent can adjust ticket prices dynamically based on demand, time of travel, and seat availability, maximizing revenue and profitability for railway operators. Further enhancements could include incorporating additional features such as competitor pricing and passenger demographics to improve pricing strategies and customer satisfaction. Additionally, deploying the trained model to a real-time system would enable continuous optimization of ticket prices in live railway operations.

CASE STUDY: PREDICTIVE MAINTENANCE FOR RAILWAY TRACKS USING MACHINE LEARNING

Background:
Railway tracks are subject to wear and tear due to various factors such as weather conditions, train loads, and material degradation. Predictive maintenance can help railway operators identify potential track defects before they lead to disruptions or accidents, ensuring the safety and reliability of train operations. In this case study, we'll develop a predictive maintenance system using machine learning to detect track defects and schedule maintenance proactively.

Objective:
To develop a predictive maintenance system that analyzes sensor data from railway tracks to predict track defects and recommend maintenance actions.

Solution:
We'll use Python and scikit-learn to implement a machine

learning model for predictive maintenance. We'll preprocess sensor data, train the machine learning model, and evaluate its performance. Finally, we'll deploy the model to make real-time predictions and schedule maintenance activities.

Python Code:

```python
import pandas as pd
from sklearn.model_selection import train_test_split
from sklearn.ensemble import RandomForestClassifier
from sklearn.metrics import accuracy_score, classification_report

# Load sensor data from railway tracks
sensor_data = pd.read_csv('railway_track_sensor_data.csv')

# Preprocess data
# (For demonstration purposes, preprocessing steps such as feature engineering and missing value imputation are assumed)

# Define features and target variable
X = sensor_data.drop(columns=['defect'])
y = sensor_data['defect']

# Split data into training and testing sets
X_train, X_test, y_train, y_test = train_test_split(X, y, test_size=0.2, random_state=42)

# Train machine learning model (Random Forest classifier)
model = RandomForestClassifier(n_estimators=100, random_state=42)
model.fit(X_train, y_train)

# Make predictions
y_pred = model.predict(X_test)

# Evaluate model performance
accuracy = accuracy_score(y_test, y_pred)
print("Accuracy:", accuracy)
```

```
report = classification_report(y_test, y_pred)
print("Classification Report:\n", report)

# Deploy model for real-time predictions and maintenance
scheduling
# (For demonstration purposes, deployment to a real-time
system is assumed)
` ` `
```

Explanation:
- We import necessary libraries including pandas, scikit-learn
for data manipulation, and machine learning.
- We load sensor data from railway tracks from a CSV file
(`railway_track_sensor_data.csv`).
- We preprocess the data, which typically includes steps such
as feature engineering and missing value imputation. However,
the specific preprocessing steps are assumed for demonstration
purposes.
- We define features (sensor readings) and the target variable
(track defects).
- We split the data into training and testing sets using
`train_test_split`.
- We train a machine learning model using a Random Forest
classifier with 100 trees.
- After training, we make predictions on the testing set
and evaluate the model's performance using accuracy and
classification report.
- Finally, we deploy the trained model for real-time predictions
and maintenance scheduling, assuming deployment to a real-
time system.

Conclusion:
In this case study, we developed a predictive maintenance
system for railway tracks using machine learning. By analyzing
sensor data from railway tracks, the machine learning
model can detect potential track defects and recommend

maintenance actions proactively. This approach helps railway operators to identify and address track defects before they lead to disruptions or accidents, ensuring the safety and reliability of train operations. Further enhancements could include incorporating additional sensor data sources, exploring different machine learning algorithms, and integrating the system with existing railway maintenance workflows for seamless deployment and operation.

CASE STUDY: PASSENGER FLOW OPTIMIZATION IN RAILWAY STATIONS USING COMPUTER VISION

Background:
Efficient management of passenger flow within railway stations is crucial for ensuring smooth operations and enhancing the overall passenger experience. Traditional methods of monitoring passenger flow often rely on manual observation or static sensors, which may not provide real-time insights or accurate data. In this case study, we'll develop a system using computer vision to optimize passenger flow in railway stations by analyzing crowd movement patterns.

Objective:
To develop a computer vision-based system that analyzes video feeds from railway stations to monitor passenger flow, detect congestion areas, and optimize crowd management strategies.

Solution:
We'll use Python and OpenCV library to implement a

computer vision system for passenger flow optimization. We'll extract features such as pedestrian count, flow direction, and congestion levels from video feeds, train machine learning models for crowd analysis, and visualize insights for station managers to make informed decisions.

Python Code:

```python
import cv2
import numpy as np

# Load video feed from railway station
cap = cv2.VideoCapture('railway_station_feed.mp4')

# Initialize background subtractor
fgbg = cv2.createBackgroundSubtractorMOG2()

while True:
    ret, frame = cap.read()
    if not ret:
        break

    # Apply background subtraction to detect moving objects
    fgmask = fgbg.apply(frame)

    # Apply morphological operations to remove noise
    kernel = np.ones((5, 5), np.uint8)
    fgmask = cv2.morphologyEx(fgmask, cv2.MORPH_OPEN, kernel)

    # Find contours of moving objects
    contours, _ = cv2.findContours(fgmask, cv2.RETR_EXTERNAL, cv2.CHAIN_APPROX_SIMPLE)

    # Analyze pedestrian count and flow direction
    pedestrian_count = len(contours)
    for contour in contours:
        # Calculate centroid of each contour
        M = cv2.moments(contour)
```

```
        cx = int(M['m10'] / M['m00'])
        cy = int(M['m01'] / M['m00'])

        # Perform flow direction analysis based on centroid
position

        # Perform congestion analysis

        # Update passenger flow visualization

    # Display processed frame
    cv2.imshow('Passenger Flow Analysis', frame)

    if cv2.waitKey(1) & 0xFF == ord('q'):
        break

cap.release()
cv2.destroyAllWindows()
```
```

Explanation:
- We import the necessary libraries including OpenCV for computer vision.
- We load the video feed from the railway station using `cv2.VideoCapture`.
- We initialize a background subtractor to detect moving objects (pedestrians).
- We apply background subtraction and morphological operations to the frame to extract moving objects (foreground mask).
- We find contours of the moving objects using `cv2.findContours`.
- We analyze pedestrian count, flow direction, and congestion levels based on contour properties such as centroid position.
- We update passenger flow visualization with insights obtained from the analysis.
- Finally, we display the processed frame with passenger flow visualization using `cv2.imshow`.
```

Conclusion:
In this case study, we developed a computer vision-based system for optimizing passenger flow in railway stations. By analyzing video feeds from railway stations, the system can monitor passenger movement, detect congestion areas, and provide insights for optimizing crowd management strategies. This approach helps railway operators to improve the efficiency of passenger flow, reduce congestion, and enhance the overall passenger experience within railway stations. Further enhancements could include incorporating advanced machine learning models for crowd analysis, integrating the system with real-time data streams for dynamic optimization, and deploying the system to multiple railway stations for broader impact.

CASE STUDY: ROUTE OPTIMIZATION FOR RAILWAY FREIGHT USING GENETIC ALGORITHM

Background:
Efficient routing of railway freight is essential for minimizing transportation costs, reducing delivery times, and maximizing resource utilization. Traditional routing methods often rely on manual planning or heuristic algorithms, which may not always produce optimal solutions, especially for complex networks. In this case study, we'll develop a route optimization system using a genetic algorithm to find optimal freight routes for railway transportation.

Objective:
To develop a genetic algorithm-based system that optimizes freight routes for railway transportation, considering factors such as distance, capacity, and delivery deadlines.

Solution:
We'll use Python and the DEAP library (Distributed Evolutionary Algorithms in Python) to implement a genetic algorithm for route optimization. We'll define chromosome representation, fitness evaluation, selection, crossover, and mutation

operations to evolve optimal freight routes.

Python Code:
```python
import random
import numpy as np
from deap import base, creator, tools

# Define route optimization problem parameters
NUM_TRAINS = 20
NUM_NODES = 50
MAX_CAPACITY = 100
MAX_DISTANCE = 500
DELIVERY_DEADLINE = 24 * 7  # 1 week

# Define chromosome representation
creator.create("FitnessMax", base.Fitness, weights=(1.0,))
creator.create("Individual", list, fitness=creator.FitnessMax)

toolbox = base.Toolbox()

toolbox.register("attr_int", random.randint, 0, NUM_NODES-1)
# Node index
toolbox.register("individual", tools.initRepeat,
creator.Individual, toolbox.attr_int, n=NUM_TRAINS)
toolbox.register("population", tools.initRepeat, list,
toolbox.individual)

# Define fitness evaluation function
def evaluate(individual):
    # Placeholder fitness evaluation function
    # Fitness could be based on factors such as total distance,
delivery deadline compliance, and capacity utilization
    return (np.sum(individual),)

toolbox.register("evaluate", evaluate)

# Define genetic operators
toolbox.register("mate", tools.cxTwoPoint)
```

```python
toolbox.register("mutate",    tools.mutUniformInt,    low=0,
up=NUM_NODES-1, indpb=0.05)
toolbox.register("select", tools.selTournament, tournsize=3)

# Define main evolutionary algorithm
def main():
    # Initialize population
    population = toolbox.population(n=100)

    # Evaluate fitness of initial population
    fitnesses = list(map(toolbox.evaluate, population))
    for ind, fit in zip(population, fitnesses):
        ind.fitness.values = fit

    # Define evolutionary parameters
    CXPB, MUTPB, NGEN = 0.5, 0.2, 50

    # Evolution loop
    for gen in range(NGEN):
        # Select the next generation individuals
        offspring = toolbox.select(population, len(population))
        # Clone selected individuals
        offspring = list(map(toolbox.clone, offspring))

        # Apply crossover and mutation on offspring
        for child1, child2 in zip(offspring[::2], offspring[1::2]):
            if random.random() < CXPB:
                toolbox.mate(child1, child2)
                del child1.fitness.values
                del child2.fitness.values

        for mutant in offspring:
            if random.random() < MUTPB:
                toolbox.mutate(mutant)
                del mutant.fitness.values

        # Evaluate fitness of offspring
        invalid_ind = [ind for ind in offspring if not
ind.fitness.valid]
```

```
        fitnesses = map(toolbox.evaluate, invalid_ind)
        for ind, fit in zip(invalid_ind, fitnesses):
            ind.fitness.values = fit

        # Replace population with offspring
        population[:] = offspring

        # Print best individual in current generation
        print("Generation:",        gen,       "Best        Fitness:",
    max([ind.fitness.values[0] for ind in population]))

    if __name__ == "__main__":
        main()
    ` ` `
```

Explanation:
- We import necessary libraries including random and numpy for random number generation and array manipulation, and DEAP for genetic algorithm implementation.
- We define a custom chromosome representation using integer values representing node indices for freight route selection.
- We create a DEAP creator for defining the fitness function and individual representation.
- We define the fitness evaluation function to evaluate the fitness of individuals based on factors such as total distance, delivery deadline compliance, and capacity utilization.
- We register genetic operators including selection, crossover, and mutation.
- We implement the main evolutionary algorithm loop, which includes selection, crossover, mutation, fitness evaluation, and replacement steps.
- The algorithm evolves a population of individuals over multiple generations, aiming to maximize the fitness of the individuals representing optimal freight routes.

Conclusion:
In this case study, we developed a genetic algorithm-based system for optimizing freight routes for railway transportation.

By evolving optimal routes through selection, crossover, and mutation operations, the system can efficiently allocate resources, minimize transportation costs, and meet delivery deadlines. Further enhancements could include incorporating additional constraints such as station capacities and train schedules, and integrating the system with real-time data for dynamic route optimization in live railway operations.

CASE STUDY: REAL-TIME RAILWAY SCHEDULE OPTIMIZATION USING REINFORCEMENT LEARNING

Background:
Efficient scheduling of trains is crucial for maintaining smooth operations, minimizing delays, and maximizing resource utilization in railway networks. Traditional scheduling methods often rely on static timetables, which may not adapt well to dynamic changes in demand and network conditions. In this case study, we'll develop a real-time schedule optimization system using reinforcement learning to dynamically adjust train schedules based on real-time data and passenger demand.

Objective:
To develop a reinforcement learning-based system that optimizes train schedules in real-time, considering factors such as passenger demand, track capacity, and delays.

Solution:
We'll use Python and the Stable Baselines library to implement

a reinforcement learning environment and train a Deep Q-Network (DQN) agent for real-time schedule optimization. The agent will learn optimal actions (train schedules) based on observations of network conditions and historical data.

Python Code:
```python
import gym
from stable_baselines3 import DQN
from stable_baselines3.common.vec_env import DummyVecEnv
import numpy as np

class RailwayScheduleEnv(gym.Env):
    def __init__(self):
        super(RailwayScheduleEnv, self).__init__()
        # Define action space (train schedules)
        self.action_space = gym.spaces.Discrete(NUM_SCHEDULES)

        # Define observation space (network conditions, passenger demand, etc.)
        self.observation_space = gym.spaces.Box(low=0, high=1, shape=(NUM_FEATURES,), dtype=np.float32)

        # Initialize state
        self.state = self.observation_space.sample()

    def reset(self):
        # Reset state to initial state
        self.state = self.observation_space.sample()
        return self.state

    def step(self, action):
        # Simulate train scheduling and calculate reward
        reward = self._calculate_reward(action)

        # Simulate state transition based on action
        self.state = self.observation_space.sample()  # Placeholder
```

for dynamic state transition

```
        return self.state, reward, False, {}

    def _calculate_reward(self, action):
        # Placeholder reward calculation function
        # Reward could be based on factors such as passenger
satisfaction, on-time performance, and resource utilization
        return np.random.uniform(0, 100)   # Example: random
reward

# Create railway schedule environment
env = DummyVecEnv([lambda: RailwayScheduleEnv()])

# Train DQN agent
model = DQN("MlpPolicy", env, verbose=1)
model.learn(total_timesteps=10000)

# Deploy trained model for real-time schedule optimization
# (For demonstration purposes, deployment to a real-time
system is assumed)
```
```

Explanation:
- We import necessary libraries including gym and Stable Baselines for reinforcement learning.
- We define a custom Gym environment, `RailwayScheduleEnv`, for the railway schedule optimization problem.
- We implement the `step` method to simulate train scheduling, state transitions, and calculate rewards based on actions.
- We define discrete action space for train schedules and continuous observation space for network conditions and passenger demand.
- We create the railway schedule environment and train a Deep Q-Network (DQN) agent using the Stable Baselines library.
- After training, we can deploy the trained model for real-time
```

schedule optimization, assuming deployment to a real-time system.

Conclusion:
In this case study, we developed a reinforcement learning-based system for real-time railway schedule optimization. By learning optimal actions (train schedules) based on observations of network conditions and historical data, the Deep Q-Network (DQN) agent can dynamically adjust train schedules to meet passenger demand, minimize delays, and maximize resource utilization in railway networks. Further enhancements could include incorporating additional features such as weather conditions and track maintenance schedules, and integrating the system with real-time data streams for dynamic optimization in live railway operations.

CASE STUDY: PREDICTING RAILWAY EQUIPMENT FAILURES WITH MACHINE LEARNING

Background:
Predictive maintenance is critical for ensuring the reliability and safety of railway operations. By identifying potential equipment failures before they occur, maintenance activities can be scheduled proactively, minimizing downtime and reducing operational costs. In this case study, we'll develop a predictive maintenance system using machine learning to forecast equipment failures in railway infrastructure.

Objective:
To develop a machine learning model that predicts equipment failures in railway infrastructure based on historical maintenance data and sensor readings.

Solution:
We'll use Python and scikit-learn to implement a machine learning pipeline for predicting equipment failures. We'll preprocess historical maintenance data and sensor readings, train a machine learning model, and evaluate its performance in terms of predictive accuracy.

Python Code:
```python
import pandas as pd
from sklearn.model_selection import train_test_split
from sklearn.ensemble import RandomForestClassifier
from sklearn.metrics import classification_report

# Load historical maintenance data and sensor readings
maintenance_data = pd.read_csv('maintenance_data.csv')
sensor_readings = pd.read_csv('sensor_readings.csv')

# Merge maintenance data and sensor readings
merged_data = pd.merge(maintenance_data, sensor_readings,
on='equipment_id', how='inner')

# Preprocess data
# (For demonstration purposes, preprocessing steps such as
feature engineering and missing value imputation are assumed)

# Define features and target variable
X = merged_data.drop(columns=['failure'])
y = merged_data['failure']

# Split data into training and testing sets
X_train, X_test, y_train, y_test = train_test_split(X, y,
test_size=0.2, random_state=42)

# Train machine learning model (Random Forest classifier)
model = RandomForestClassifier(n_estimators=100,
random_state=42)
model.fit(X_train, y_train)

# Make predictions
y_pred = model.predict(X_test)

# Evaluate model performance
report = classification_report(y_test, y_pred)
print("Classification Report:\n", report)
```

Explanation:
- We import necessary libraries including pandas, scikit-learn for data manipulation, and machine learning.
- We load historical maintenance data and sensor readings from CSV files (`maintenance_data.csv` and `sensor_readings.csv`).
- We merge the maintenance data and sensor readings based on equipment ID to create a single dataset.
- We preprocess the merged data, which may include steps such as feature engineering, encoding categorical variables, and handling missing values.
- We define features (sensor readings, maintenance history) and the target variable (equipment failure).
- We split the data into training and testing sets using `train_test_split`.
- We train a machine learning model using a Random Forest classifier with 100 trees.
- After training, we make predictions on the testing set and evaluate the model's performance using classification report.

Conclusion:
In this case study, we developed a machine learning-based predictive maintenance system for railway equipment failures. By analyzing historical maintenance data and sensor readings, the machine learning model can predict equipment failures before they occur, enabling proactive maintenance activities and minimizing downtime in railway operations. Further enhancements could include incorporating additional sensor data sources, exploring different machine learning algorithms, and integrating the system with real-time monitoring for continuous predictive maintenance in live railway operations.

CASE STUDY: DYNAMIC PRICING OPTIMIZATION FOR RAILWAY TICKETS USING REINFORCEMENT LEARNING

Background:
Dynamic pricing is a strategy widely used across various industries, including transportation, to optimize revenue by adjusting prices based on demand, time of booking, and other factors. In the railway industry, dynamic pricing can help maximize revenue while ensuring optimal utilization of available seats. In this case study, we'll develop a dynamic pricing optimization system for railway tickets using reinforcement learning.

Objective:
To develop a dynamic pricing optimization system using reinforcement learning that adjusts ticket prices in real-time based on demand and other factors.

Solution:

We'll use Python and the TensorFlow library to implement a reinforcement learning agent that learns to optimize ticket prices for railway journeys. The agent will interact with the environment, observe demand patterns, and adjust prices accordingly to maximize revenue.

Python Code:

```python
import numpy as np
import tensorflow as tf

class DynamicPricingAgent:
    def __init__(self, num_prices, learning_rate=0.001, gamma=0.99, epsilon=1.0, epsilon_decay=0.999, epsilon_min=0.01):
        self.num_prices = num_prices
        self.learning_rate = learning_rate
        self.gamma = gamma
        self.epsilon = epsilon
        self.epsilon_decay = epsilon_decay
        self.epsilon_min = epsilon_min

        self.model = self.build_model()
        self.optimizer = tf.keras.optimizers.Adam(learning_rate=self.learning_rate)

    def build_model(self):
        model = tf.keras.Sequential([
            tf.keras.layers.Dense(128, activation='relu', input_shape=(self.num_prices,)),
            tf.keras.layers.Dense(64, activation='relu'),
            tf.keras.layers.Dense(self.num_prices)
        ])
        return model

    def get_action(self, state):
```

```
    if np.random.rand() <= self.epsilon:
        return np.random.randint(self.num_prices)
    else:
        q_values = self.model.predict(state)
        return np.argmax(q_values[0])

def train(self, state, action, reward, next_state, done):
    if done:
        target = reward
    else:
        target = reward + self.gamma * np.max(self.model.predict(next_state)[0])

    with tf.GradientTape() as tape:
        q_values = self.model(state, training=True)
        action_values = q_values[0][action]
        loss = tf.reduce_mean(tf.square(target - action_values))

    grads = tape.gradient(loss, self.model.trainable_variables)
    self.optimizer.apply_gradients(zip(grads, self.model.trainable_variables))

    if self.epsilon > self.epsilon_min:
        self.epsilon *= self.epsilon_decay
```

Explanation:
- We define a `DynamicPricingAgent` class that encapsulates the functionality of our reinforcement learning agent.
- The agent's neural network model takes the number of available price levels as input and outputs the estimated Q-values for each action (price level).
- The `get_action` method selects an action based on an ε-greedy policy, allowing for exploration.
- The `train` method updates the agent's neural network parameters using the Q-learning algorithm and a mean squared error loss function.

Conclusion:

In this case study, we developed a dynamic pricing optimization system for railway tickets using reinforcement learning. By training a reinforcement learning agent to adjust ticket prices based on demand and other factors, railway operators can maximize revenue and optimize resource utilization. Further enhancements could include incorporating additional features such as time of booking, passenger preferences, and competitor pricing, as well as deploying the system in real-world railway ticketing platforms for live testing and optimization.

CASE STUDY: REAL-TIME PASSENGER FLOW MONITORING USING COMPUTER VISION

Background:
Efficient management of passenger flow is essential for ensuring smooth operations and enhancing the overall experience in transportation hubs such as railway stations. Traditional methods of monitoring passenger flow often rely on manual observation or static sensors, which may not provide real-time insights or accurate data. In this case study, we'll develop a real-time passenger flow monitoring system using computer vision to analyze video feeds from railway stations.

Objective:
To develop a computer vision-based system that monitors passenger flow in real-time at railway stations, detects congestion areas, and provides insights for crowd management.

Solution:
We'll use Python and the OpenCV library to implement a computer vision system for real-time passenger flow monitoring. The system will analyze video feeds from surveillance cameras, detect individuals, track their

movements, and visualize passenger flow patterns.

Python Code:
```python
import cv2
import numpy as np

# Load pre-trained pedestrian detection model
hog = cv2.HOGDescriptor()
hog.setSVMDetector(cv2.HOGDescriptor_getDefaultPeopleDetector())

# Open video feed from railway station
cap = cv2.VideoCapture('railway_station_feed.mp4')

while True:
    ret, frame = cap.read()
    if not ret:
        break

    # Convert frame to grayscale for pedestrian detection
    gray = cv2.cvtColor(frame, cv2.COLOR_BGR2GRAY)

    # Detect pedestrians in the frame
    boxes, weights = hog.detectMultiScale(gray, winStride=(8, 8))

    # Draw bounding boxes around detected pedestrians
    for (x, y, w, h) in boxes:
        cv2.rectangle(frame, (x, y), (x + w, y + h), (0, 255, 0), 2)

    # Display frame with pedestrian detection
    cv2.imshow('Passenger Flow Monitoring', frame)

    if cv2.waitKey(1) & 0xFF == ord('q'):
        break

cap.release()
cv2.destroyAllWindows()
```

Explanation:

- We use the Histogram of Oriented Gradients (HOG) algorithm for pedestrian detection, which is a commonly used method for detecting humans in images.
- We load a pre-trained pedestrian detection model using the HOGDescriptor class in OpenCV.
- We open a video feed from a railway station using the VideoCapture class in OpenCV.
- In each frame of the video feed, we convert the frame to grayscale and apply pedestrian detection using the detectMultiScale method of the HOG descriptor.
- Detected pedestrians are represented as bounding boxes, which are drawn on the frame using the rectangle method in OpenCV.
- Finally, we display the frame with pedestrian detection using the imshow method in OpenCV.

Conclusion:
In this case study, we developed a real-time passenger flow monitoring system using computer vision. By analyzing video feeds from railway stations and detecting pedestrians in real-time, the system can provide insights into passenger flow patterns, identify congestion areas, and assist in crowd management strategies. Further enhancements could include integrating the system with advanced algorithms for pedestrian tracking, density estimation, and crowd behavior analysis to provide more comprehensive insights for railway station operators.